THE DRAMA
OF
THE END-TIME

by
Oral Roberts

Contents

CHAPTER ONE

Signs of the Last Days

WHAT LIES JUST AHEAD? Where are we bound? What will be the next event? Is Jesus returning soon? Are there any new signs?

Such are the questions that are uppermost in the minds of thinking people everywhere. Men know not which way to turn. Nations are perplexed; great leaders are baffled. The United Nations is unceasingly harassed by almost impossible world problems. Marked uncertainty is everywhere. Mistrust hampers any real progress at the disarmament negotiations.

Can anyone doubt that we are living in the last days? The rumbling of the distant kingdom of Antichrist can plainly be heard. We are on the eve of something awesome, and we can feel it.

The tide of sin in the world is so great that it seems that the worst in man is now being manifested. Every conceivable sin is being committed as crime rates reach most disturbing proportions. Communistic Russia and China threaten to bury the world, be it by their euphemistic "peaceful coexistence" or by their localized wars. Disregarding the protests of the world, the Soviet Union recently set off a nuclear blast with a force greater than 55 megatons. It was reported that this had the explosive power of 55-million tons of TNT, almost 3,000 times the destructive force of the infant A-bomb which was dropped on Hiroshima to end World War II. Multitudes are living in a gnawing dread of greater calamities and disasters. What next?

We are nearing the end of this age. An age that shall end in chaos, despair and destruction for the sinful element of the world. The climax of man's sinful rule will result in the Battle of Armageddon, the coming of Christ in power and glory, the defeat of Satan's forces and the reign of the Lord Jesus Christ with His redeemed. The nearer we approach the end, the worse the age will become.

Before the judgment of the flood, God saw that the wickedness of man was great in the earth and that every imagination of the thoughts of his heart was only evil continually. The world had come to a climax in its thinking—people had totally rejected God. Noah had come to a climax in his thinking—he had totally accepted God. The climax for both had occurred simultaneously.

God made a pronouncement. He said, "My spirit shall not always strive with man . . . yet his days shall be an hundred and twenty years." God placed a time limit of 120 years upon man's life. And during that time, man was given the opportunity to hear the Word of God.

As Noah walked with God, he served as a constant warning

to the world of coming judgment. Before the end of a 120 years, Noah had constructed a huge vessel, large enough to accommodate every living thing that would respond to God. The animals of the fields and forests and the fowls of the air heard the voice of God and they came. Then Noah's family entered the ark and God shut the door.

Before the rains came, seven last precious days of grace were spurned by the scoffing and rejecting world of unbelievers. Then it started. It began to rain, something it had never done before in the history of the world. The lightning flashed, the thunder roared, all the fountains of the great deep burst forth as the windows of heaven were opened. The rain came in driving sheets. It covered the ground. It filled the earth. It rose above the highest hill. And every living thing except those in the ark was destroyed. When enough sin fills the earth, a point of saturation is reached. It brought a deluge the first time; what will happen the next time?

In this age, the climax of man's sin shall upset the delicate balance of the groaning creation, thereby releasing a terrible nuclear chain reaction that shall ultimately reduce to ashes every living thing that is not of God. (Revelation 20:9.)

When the world makes up its mind, totally rejecting God, I believe that at that exact time the people of God shall have made up their minds to totally accept God. There will be a simultaneous climax of the persuasion of the world and God's people. When that happens, two things will take place.

First, the climax of the acceptance of God's people will cause Christ to return. That is the great day when Jesus suddenly and secretly comes for His people. The climax of the world's rejection of Christ will produce the Antichrist, the

Mark of the Beast, the Tribulation, the Battle of Armageddon and the fiery destruction of the armies of the world from the presence of God.

In receiving mail from people all over the world, I am asked almost continually, "Brother Roberts, do you believe in the Second Coming of Jesus Christ? If you do, how will He come? When will He come? Where will He come? What will be the manner of His coming?"

Those answers are found in God's Book. God has known the end from the beginning. Prophecy is history written in advance. And to those who diligently study God's Word, the future is an open book. Future events spread out before our gaze in a grand panorama, giving us a view, one by one, of the things that must shortly come to pass as told in God's Word. What God's prophets have written will happen. Consequently, the Bible is the only book that adequately explains the future; it alone has the key to the perplexing problems that are now facing us.

Jesus, in anticipation of the troublesome events of the end-time, had this to add in way of comfort to His redeemed people, "When these things begin to come to pass, then look up, and lift up your heads; for your redemption draweth nigh" (Luke 21:28). Over and over we are told that He is coming! Thank God, with heads high and souls lifted up in heavenly strength, Spirit-filled believers are expecting, watching and waiting.

We are told also that Antichrist shall come. In due time, this person will appear with enticing words of man's wisdom and Satanic wisdom with which to cope with world problems. He will deal with the perplexing problems and dilemmas of the day. He will be heralded as the champion of human interests and the savior of the world. Poverty will be seemingly wiped out, giving way to a new order. For a time there will be plenty of money and an abundance of work. None shall be idle for lack of employment. Rich and poor alike shall come under his power and fall under his sway. And then it will be discovered that he is the Antichrist of prophecy. The world will realize that its new god, its fascinating, powerful ruler is none other than the mad Beast of hell in the form of a man.

The question arises, How near are we to Christ's coming, Antichrist's appearing, and Tribulation horrors? What do the Scriptures say about these coming events? Are there any new signs to indicate that these last-day events are near? Definitely, yes. There are many special end-time signs recorded in God's Word. We, of this generation, are seeing a more rapid fulfillment of these signs than any preceding one. Many have never before appeared on the earth, but we need not be ignorant, we should not be in the dark. The future is being unveiled by our God and we know something of what is to come.

I want to point out to you some definite signs of the last days that are now appearing and make a few comments on them. Let us see what they are.

1. THE RETURN OF THE JEWS TO PALESTINE

The Jews are a distinct and separate people. They are, without doubt, the most remarkable people in all the world. For centuries they have been scattered, persecuted and cruelly treated. No people have ever suffered so much as the Jews. Shudder at the inhuman slaughter of six million Jews by twentieth century Eichmanns under Hitlerian dictatorship. Yet the Jews are destined to play a leading part in the drama of the end-time. They are yet God's ancient people and a great God-planned destiny awaits them.

When Jesus was on earth, He said, "Now learn a parable of the fig tree; When his branch is yet tender, and putteth forth leaves, ye know that summer is nigh. So likewise ye, when ye shall see all these things, know that it is near, even at the doors" (Matthew 24:32, 33). God compares the Jewish people to a fig tree and in this passage He tells us that when the fig tree begins to bud we are nearing the end-time. Nearly all Bible scholars are in agreement that the budding of the fig tree and the shooting forth of its branches are a type of the Jews returning to their homeland.

Although the Jews have been scattered over the world, they have not been assimilated by the nations nor have they lost their racial distinctiveness. They have been persecuted by the Pharaohs, the Nebuchadnezzars, the Hamans and Hitlers of history. Still the Jew has survived.

Shortly after the atomic era began, the nation of Israel was reborn on May 14, 1948. The dream, for which Jews had prayed 1,900 years, was at last a reality. The fulfillment of faith and prophecy could no longer be frustrated. The flag of David was lifted in the nation for the first time since Titus removed it in AD 70. But Israel is destined to go through its worst baptism of suffering—the Great Tribulation. "Alas! for that day is great, so that none is like it: it is even the time of Jacob's trouble; but he shall be saved out of it" (Jeremiah 30:7). They shall experience the Tribulation, a time of trouble and terror.

In the middle of the Tribulation, Antichrist shall break his covenant with Israel. "And he shall confirm the covenant with many for one week: and in the midst of the week he shall cause the sacrifice and the oblation to cease . . ." (Daniel 9:27). The daily sacrifice will cease. Antichrist shall desecrate the temple (the abomination of desolation) and set up a reign of terror against God's people that shall have no parallel in history. It will end in the Battle of Armageddon at which time the Jews shall see clearer than ever before. With eyes opened, they shall believe on the name of Jesus Christ and shall accept Him as the Messiah.

2. A WIDESPREAD, DEEP-SEATED DEPARTURE FROM GOD

"That day shall not come," said Apostle Paul, "except there come a falling away first, and that man of sin be revealed" (2 Thessalonians 2:3).

"Now the Spirit speaketh expressly, that in the latter times some shall depart from the faith, giving heed to seducing spirits and doctrines of devils" (1 Timothy 4:1).

"They shall turn away their ears from the truth" (2 Timothy 4:4).

"And many false prophets shall rise, and shall deceive many" (Matthew 24:11).

Many who once believed the fundamental doctrines of God's Word have now turned away from the truth. As a result, millions merely profess religion. They have not been called to paths of repentance, nor urged to forsake sin. The Christ of Calvary as Saviour and Healer has been obscured. Instead, there is churchianity without Christianity, the letter without the Spirit, the form without the power.

There is a deep-running stream of materialism in the world today. It is not enough for you and me to have a beautiful church. We must have the Spirit of Christ in us. We must be able to differentiate between faith and compromise, between what God offers and what the world offers, between truth and falsehood. And where truth is rejected, error is received.

There are people who are so cold in their reasoning that they feel they can't have faith. And because they don't get what faith will bring, they surround themselves with all kinds of ideologies and philosophies and ways of life which they substitute for the real salvation and power of God.

Does Christ offer a different philosophy, theology, doctrine or way of life today? Would He practice another form of dealing with the people other than the one that He manifested nearly 2,000 years ago? I believe He would be exactly the same today as He was then.

Jesus would urge people to clean up their lives, to clean up their hypocrisy, their adultery, their fornication, to separate themselves from this present evil and wicked world. There are thousands of backsliders who have departed from the faith. They have hardened their hearts and have turned a deaf ear to the truth. One of the saddest things to see is a man once on fire for God, now cooled off. There is a devil against humanity, against you and against me. Through many false prophets, Satan is misleading and preparing the way for the Antichrist.

The nearer we approach the Tribulation, the greater will be the appearance of apostasy.

3. INIQUITY SHALL ABOUND MORE AND MORE

It seems that lawlessness and crime have already gone as far as they can. But sin will abound in ever-increasing measure as the end draws near.

There is to be a repetition of the antediluvian and Sodomite conditions on the earth. (Luke 17:26-30; Genesis 6:5, 11-13.)

Recently, the Homosexual League of America protested that they, as a minority, were not receiving their share of air time from our radio stations. One Eastern station programmed a panel to air their premise that they are normal people who deserve acceptance and good standing in the community!

In America's sex crisis, we have high percentage increases in illegitimacy. It is reported that over one million abortions are performed each year.

Films are garishly advertised as lustful sensationalism. Perversion, degeneration, desecration and violence abound. Even some films using Biblical titles are sordid and utterly depraved. The public has been numbed to insensitivity.

Need I mention the army of juvenile delinquents? Dope addictions, sadistic violence, and thrill killing make many city dwellers afraid to leave their homes after dark. Rumbles, gang wars—boys and girls madly fighting to kill or to be killed.

Each year a billion dollars in cash and goods are stolen from companies by their own employees. Graft and corruption in government are considered normal in many countries.

Yes, sin shall abound in the last days.

4. NATIONAL DISTRESS AND
WORLD PERPLEXITY

Jesus has told us that there shall be ". . . upon the earth distress of nations, with perplexity . . . men's hearts failing them for fear, and for looking after those things which are coming on the earth; for the powers of heaven shall be shaken" (Luke 21:25, 26).

The problems of the day are baffling to the great leaders. No one seems to know just what to do. We've never seen so much sickness, so many with heart attacks. The stress and strain of this twentieth century living is more than many can bear.

In our day, one H-bomb can destroy a city—any city. We are preparing with a mass shelter program. Our Abundant Life Building in Tulsa has been included as a fallout shelter. President Kennedy, in an address to the United Nations, stated that nuclear war may start "at any moment by accident, miscalculation, or madness." In a televised review of his first two years in the White House, Mr. Kennedy said, "Once he (Khrushchev) fires his missiles, it is all over anyway, because we are going to have sufficient resources to fire back at him to destroy the Soviet Union. When that day comes, and there is a massive exchange, then that is the end, because you are talking about Western Europe, the Soviet Union, the United States, of 150-million fatalities in the first 18 hours." More distressing is the fact that the radioactive dust from a cobalt bomb would kill most life as it crosses a continent. Today we must live with new terms such as *overkill* and *megadeath*. There appears to be no practical program that would avoid large scale loss of life.

5. A FALSE PEACE

Amidst phrases such as "better Red than dead" and "better dead than Red" is the hope to be neither Red nor dead.

During the 17 nation disarmament conferences held in Geneva, the West joined the Soviet Union in a moratorium on testing. For three years the world enjoyed the cessation of nuclear testing. This brief respite ended when Russia began exploding the most powerful bombs ever set off by human hands.

With the adversary misinterpreting intentions, with a world whose mind is full of suspicion, there is a climate of hot and cold wars in this age. When a fresh outbreak occurs it is hardly news anymore, other than the fact that a new arrow pierces the heart of people everywhere.

Since 1948 there have been at least 15 official bilateral negotiations between the United States and the Soviet Union, generally on the subject of the nuclear arms race. No effective agreement has been reached on this all-important matter.

By their own definition, Russia's "peaceful coexistence" means the prosecution of their offensive toward world domination by all means short of the general war that would be self-defeating.

"For when they shall say, Peace and safety; then sudden destruction cometh upon them" (1 Thessalonians 5:3). The United Nations continues to exist because of man's desperate hope for peace. But there will be no abiding peace in this world until Jesus comes back to this earth to be its King forever.

6. INCREASE OF KNOWLEDGE—TRAVEL

"But thou, O Daniel, shut up the words, and seal the book, even to the time of the end: many shall run to and fro, and knowledge shall be increased" (Daniel 12:4).

When I was a child, the means of transportation were very poor and limited. Today, everyone seems to travel—and fast. Whereas we used to travel by foot or in a wagon along muddy roads, now it's in a high-powered automobile along a modern multi-laned highway. Monorails and hydrofoils speed over the traffic and water at top speeds. Far above our heads, supersonic jets which can cross the nation in little more than an hour, leave long white streaks in the sky. A number of astronauts have orbited our earth at 18,000 miles an hour, while experiencing the strange sensation of weightlessness. Our spacecraft Mariner II recently made the first close inspection of the planet Venus, 36 million miles from the earth. Our scientists expect to put several men on the moon and bring them back before this decade closes. Many shall run to and fro!

The increase of knowledge is simply wonderful. Great universities cannot keep pace with the applications for entrance. There is a teacher shortage in many cities. Unfortunately, many of these secular halls of learning permeate the young, open minds with naturalism and humanism. As a result, many possessing faith in God as they enter will leave as agnostics, ready for the philosophy of the Antichrist.

God showed me several years ago that I must undertake by faith the greatest and most far-reaching step of my ministry for the salvation of souls. That is to build the Oral Roberts

University. I feel that I am moving according to God's time-table, for God has a time for everything. In order to take the message of deliverance to my generation, I must do it not only through the seven World Outreaches and through my personal ministry, I must do it through the minds, souls and hands of others.

I believe that before the coming of the Lord we will see thousands of boys and girls suddenly filled with the Holy Spirit. They will become witnesses throughout the world. This is why we're building a major, class A academic university, where we'll turn out scientists, engineers, teachers, business people, ministers and others. The very heart of this education will be the exaltation of Jesus Christ, the baptism with the Holy Spirit, the nine gifts of the Holy Spirit, the supernatural power of God, and soul winning at the highest level. The only truly bright future belongs to the people who are truly filled with the Holy Spirit and who yield themselves to Him daily.

The coming great move of God will be a spiritual revolution throughout the earth. The Holy Spirit is going to move in the spiritual realm in a way that will overshadow the momentous success of any space penetration. Let us be reminded that our God controls the space not only in the atmosphere or in outer space but beyond all space.

Knowledge shall be increased. Never in the history of the world until this age have the prophecies of Daniel thus been fulfilled.

7. FAMINE, PESTILENCE AND EARTHQUAKES

"There shall be famines, and pestilences, and earthquakes in divers places" (Matthew 24:8).

There are thousands of earthquakes each year which are strong enough to be recorded by seismographs. On the average, ten are major earthquakes.

In our twentieth century we have witnessed death tolls of over 200,000 in Kansu, China; thousands in Messina, Italy and Tokyo, Japan, from destructive earthquakes. In the California earthquake, which was felt for a length of 750 miles, the amount of energy released by this movement was about 100,-000 times greater than that of the atomic bomb exploded over Hiroshima.

Multiplied millions in our modern times have perished in widespread famines in India, Russia and China. In 1943 there were 1½-million deaths due to famine in Bengal. After World War II, 15-million lives were saved from famine due to the effective work of the United Nations Relief and Rehabilitation Administration.

Pestilence usually follows wars and famines. Shortly after the First World War, an influenza epidemic covered the earth, wiping out over 10-million lives.

The world faces an apocalyptic inventory which can be man created by littering the sky with radioactive garbage whose seepage will infect the earth and enter human tissues. Bombs which release germs to spread killing diseases are awful realities in this closing age. Never in history has humanity as a whole marched as sheep to a slaughter. The picture is very dark, but there is a brighter view.

8. A WITNESSING, SPIRIT-FILLED CHURCH

God has shown me that men will not destroy themselves in this generation. Man will not totally annihilate the human race before the coming of Christ. In spite of his stockpiles of nuclear weapons, he will not destroy himself. That does not mean that there will be no destruction or no wars, because there will be some. But there will not be total annihilation.

Remember that where sin abounds, the grace of God does much more abound. Therefore, in this critical time, God's power is coming against the devil's power. God is giving His people knowledge of supernatural power from on high. To match the destructive nuclear weapons, God's witnessing, Spirit-filled church is to have weapons of deliverance—the nine supernatural gifts of the Holy Spirit in full operation.

God is stirring the hearts of His missionaries in all foreign lands. Mighty miracles of deliverance will arrest the heathen, and there will be a revival the like of which we've never known before in the history of the world.

I have traveled more than one million miles to preach the gospel, to win souls to Christ and to pray for the healing of the sick. I have loved every mile, every experience, every heartache, every triumph because each one has brought me closer to Christ. God has shown me that there is to be a coming together of the annointed people of God for the final revival. In the hearts of God's people there will be a kindred spirit; they will feel it and there will be a coming together of our hearts for the final revival.

God is going to intervene directly in human affairs. Mass miracles are coming to pass in large audiences. I believe this will come soon . . . very soon. As each crises builds up to greater potential dangers, the goodness of God will be leading multitudes to repentance. "And when these things begin to come to pass, then look up, and lift up your heads; for your redemption draweth nigh" (Luke 21:28). Are you ready? Are you saved by the blood of Christ? Are you doing God's work? Are you winning souls?

"Ye shall receive power, after that the Holy Ghost is come upon you: and ye shall be witnesses . . . unto the uttermost part of the earth" (Acts 1:8). Now is the time!

CHAPTER TWO

The Antichrist of Prophecy

"ANTICHRIST SHALL COME" (1 John 2:18). Such is the inspired announcement. Hence the superman for whom all the world is waiting will soon be here. Even now he may be alive. But who is he? Where does he come from? How will we recognize him? What will be the chief characteristics of his fearful reign? How soon may we expect him? Are we nearing the Great Tribulation? Is America headed for dictatorship? Is Jesus coming soon? What will happen next? Are there answers to these great questions? What saith the Scriptures? Is there an answer in the Word of God? Yes, God's Book alone holds the key. It alone can lift the veil and reveal the future. The Bible is God's forecast of the future.

The 13th Chapter of "The Revelation of Jesus Christ" gives us a vivid picture of Tribulation events. It gives us a mountain-top view of the rising of the monstrous seven-headed, ten-horned Beast, his fascinating personality, his bitter blasphemies, his deception of the nations, his persecutions against the "left ones," his worldwide dominion and universal dictatorship. Verse 9 of this great chapter says, "If any man have an ear let him hear." The Lord wants us to know what is going to happen next. He desires His people to study His prophetic Word and to be able to give an answer to all men concerning the great questions of the future. He has told us to "Study to shew thyself approved unto God, a workman that needeth not to be ashamed, rightly dividing the word of truth" (2 Timothy 2:15). Repeatedly He has urged, "Watch ye therefore, and pray always, that ye may be accounted worthy to escape all these things that shall come to pass, and to stand before the Son of man" (Luke 21:36). For the lack of faith and understanding there will be millions of human beings who will accept the leadership of Antichrist, that fearful being from hell. They will accept his soul-dooming mark, thus sealing their eternal doom forever. Men and women, God wants us to hear, to understand and to know what is going to happen in the future. Through the Scriptures we can know God's exact teaching on the appearance, the workings, the lying wonders of Antichrist and thus be in a position to meet any eventuality.

The next event on the calendar of prophecy will be the catching away or Rapture of the believers at His Second Coming. The signs of the times are being fulfilled and serve as signposts pointing to the Lord's soon return. In fact, the Scriptures indicate that the Lord Jesus is getting ready at any moment to catch away His redeemed, Spirit-filled people from this world of sin and sorrow. Many believe that Christ could come now and not destroy a single verse of prophetic Scripture that relates to the Rapture. It shall be sudden and secretive. "Watch therefore: for ye know not what hour your Lord doth come" (Matthew 24:42). The coming of the Lord remains ever imminent. The next voice we may hear could be the voice of our Saviour. "For the Lord himself shall descend from heaven with a shout . . . and the dead in Christ shall rise first: Then we which are alive and remain shall be caught up together with them in the clouds, to meet the Lord in the air" (1 Thessalonians 4:16,17).

The dead in Christ shall be raised from all the graveyards of past time, while the living shall join them in flight to meet the Lord in the air. With His Church, the Bride, Christ shall lead the way through to Heaven. There the risen redeemed shall appear before the Judgment Seat of Christ, where, upon the basis of each believers' work on earth, the rewards shall be announced. (2 Corinthians 5:8-10; 1 Corinthians 3:11-15.) Following this important event in the heavenlies, the marvelous Marriage Supper of the Lamb shall take place. (Revelation 19:7-9.)

The Bride will be caught away before the Tribulation Period begins. I believe the redeemed will taste none of its actual horrors. They shall never face Antichrist and his blasphemous mobs. The Rapture means deliverance before, and absence from the Tribulation sorrows. It behooves us as God's people to live closely to our Lord, to deny worldly lusts and to live soberly and righteously in this present world. Let us watch and pray that we might be counted worthy to escape all these dreadful things that must shortly come to pass upon the earth.

Immediately after the catching away of the redeemed Church, one of the most terrible events in the history of the world will take place. An event so dreadful, so awful that it frightens me to even think of it. The devil shall be cast out into the earth to personally take charge of the Tribulation Period.

I know, of course, that there is a tendency today to reject the teaching of the Bible regarding the existence and activity of a personal devil. But I believe God's Book just as it is and that Satan is just as real as you or I, and that he is still as active as ever. Who is the devil? There was a time when there was no devil. A being created as one of the cherubim was appointed to a position of high authority. He was one of the highest and most exalted of God's created angels. This part of his life is revealed in Ezekiel 28:12-19. Some picture him with hoofs, horns and tail. Why, I do not know. There is no such description given to him in the Bible. He was the perfection of all that was beautiful, the highest of God's creation. This passage makes it clear that he was a created being. He is not as God, from everlasting to everlasting. He was not like Christ, who was with God from the very beginning. It was his great beauty that caused his fall. His heart was lifted up. So much more beautiful was he than any other, so much more intelligent, so perfect at every point that, one day, he became proud. He began to think of himself, and finally there came the selfish realization of his great power. Then, one awful, never-to-be-forgotten day, his iniquity was discovered; and for the first time in the history of the universe there was a discordant note.

God pronounced judgment (Isaiah 14:12-17), and His messengers hastened to obey His will. God cried, "Thou shalt be brought down to hell." And in the fall of Satan we have the story of the origin of sin into the universe. For when Satan dared to say, "I will," he manifested the sin of rebellion which is, even now, hurling mankind to destruction. Satan was cast out from Heaven and thus as a spirit-being he abides in the earth's atmosphere. For thousands of years he has carried on his diabolical work against the Lord of Hosts. Therefore Paul calls him, "the prince of the power of the air" (Ephesians 2:2). On being cast out of Heaven he set about to scheme and plan the downfall of the human race which was made in the image of God. Hating this reflection of God in man, the devil grasped his opportunity to bring about the fall of man through Eve. Thus, the great battle between good and evil began. Every true believer is compelled to meet his attack. At last, in the fullness of time, Christ was born, the Son of God, whose eternal glory Satan so coveted. He struck at Him but each time he was hurled back. When Jesus died for our sins at Calvary, Satan was bruised, but not yet silenced. Now in communicating before the throne of God, Satan brazenly accuses the redeemed as he accused Job long ago. (Revelation 12:10; Job 1:6-11.) But when the Bride goes up, Satan comes down to the earth. He will be denied access to the throne of God in the Tribulation and he will accuse us no more. The battle is described in Revelation 12:7-12 as follows: "And there was war in heaven: Michael and his angels fought against the dragon; and the dragon fought and his angels, And prevailed not; neither was their place found any more in heaven. And the great dragon was cast out, that old serpent, called the Devil, and Satan, which deceiveth the whole world: he was cast out into the earth, and his angels were cast out with him. And I heard a loud voice saying in heaven, Now is come salvation, and strength, and the kingdom of our God, and the power of his Christ: for the accuser of our brethren is cast down, which accused them before our God day and night. And they overcame him by the blood of the Lamb, and by the word of their testimony; and they loved not their lives unto the death. Therefore rejoice, ye heavens, and ye that dwell in them. Woe to the inhabiters of the earth and of the sea! for the devil is come down unto you, having great wrath, because he knoweth that he hath but a short time."

Several of his names are listed here, such as, "the dragon, that old serpent, the Devil, and Satan." He is not alone; for when he was cast out, the rebellious fallen angels were cast out with him. These are aligned with Satan and faithfully obey his orders. Thus, the Great Tribulation will be introduced, in which the devil himself personally commandeers and leads. Great will be his wrath, for short will be his time. He will have only a few years in which to work. He will work feverishly. Terrible will be his ravaging, destructive activities. The dastardly plans and schemes he has employed in the past will fade away into utter insignificance as he proceeds to blot the name of God off the earth and prepares the way for his own infernal son to arise and be exalted. Satan is a spirit and can only operate in the world through the wills and minds of men; through human instrumentalities. He shall be the unseen ruler during the Tribulation. He will clandestinely operate behind the scenes. He, the great diabolical master, shall direct the activities of the last days. He will scheme and plan and at last the stage shall be set, the way prepared for the rising of the monstrous personality of the pit, the Antichrist of prophecy.

There will be living at that time a majestic being, a mighty man of cleverness and power. To this great character will Satan go and they shall enter into a conference. Satan will make an unusual offer, an offer that he has made to only one other man, the Lord Jesus Christ. Let us turn to Matthew 4:8-11 and read, "Again, the devil taketh him up into an exceeding high mountain, and sheweth him all the kingdoms of the world, and the glory of them; And saith unto him, All these things will I give thee, if thou wilt fall down and worship me. Then saith Jesus unto him, Get thee hence, Satan: for it is written, Thou shalt worship the Lord thy God, and him only shalt thou serve. Then the devil leaveth him. . . ."

This is a very important Scripture and throws much light on the way that Antichrist shall rise. The facts are that Satan sought Christ to be the Antichrist! For so doing he offered to grant Him the kingdoms of this world, which he now holds in sway, and in return Christ was to fall down and worship him. Jesus turned his offer down. Satan retreated and left Him. But this same scene shall happen again in the Tribulation, the only difference being, Christ won't be in on the subterfuge. Another person shall be sought. And on being found this personage shall enter into conference with the devil!

Think of it! A man going into conference with Satan. He shall be shown the glittering glory of this world's kingdoms. The offer Satan made to Christ will be repeated and offered to this man. Satan says, "All this will I bestow upon thee. I will glorify you with my power, crown you with the diadems of the earth's nations, and I will make you the greatest and highest honored man the world has ever known. You will be exalted. Rulers of the earth shall joyfully become your subservients. Men of renown will seek you. With my power working through you, the world shall be swept off its feet; literally captivated by your winsome personality, your majestic bearing, your marvelous power and your extraordinary intellect. All this will I give you, but on one condition. You must worship me and allow me to work my will through you. You must submit to me, your mind, soul and body; physically, emotionally, and spiritually allow me to work my will through you."

This great man shall immediately accept Satan's offer and enter into a conspiracy with the devil. Thus we read in Revelation 13:2, "And the dragon gave him his power, and his seat, and great authority." From that hour Satan will begin to lavish his mighty power upon the man who has entered into a covenant with him, the man who shall shortly usurp the power attributed to God and be recognized as the Antichrist of prophecy.

It won't be long until the political stature of this great individual will begin to enlarge. His skill, ability, and power will be increasingly displayed. Daily will he climb the ladder of influence, steadily rising higher. His shadow will be cast across the nations. His mighty figure will loom up above all earthly rulers. His fame will be spread abroad. His name will be on millions of tongues. He will be fully recognized by society. His advice will be sought by the great. International telecasts will make him the world's most popular man almost overnight. Great men will seek his counsel and wisdom as did the Queen of Sheba when she sought the counsel of King Solomon. Learned men, long skilled in diplomacy and in dealing with the human race, will be amazed at his uncanny ability, his superior wisdom, his business acumen, his capacity even for the supernatural and his intriguing, fascinating personality.

All this time Satan will be working invisibly behind the scenes. He will walk about with virtually unbridled power. With the redeemed people gone, with the Holy Spirit's restraining influence gone, remaining respect for law and decency will begin to disappear. Without the potent prayers of God's people and without the hindering influence of the Holy Spirit affecting human wills and lives, men are an easy prey for Satan. Without the convicting power of the Holy Spirit who guides into all truth, these deluded people fall victim to Satan's plans and schemes to dethrone God and glorify the Antichrist. Obeying their unbridled passion, men begin to flock to Satan's emissary. They are drawn, as it were, by an unseen force, lavishing their praise on the majestic being of sin, the Antichrist.

This great man will do mighty exploits and accomplish feat after feat. One marvelous speech after another will be made. His silver-tongued eloquence will outrival all other voices. The masses applaud and call for more. With his wonderful power of oratory, his matchless vocabulary and his winsome personality, he sweeps the world off its feet. Nations are captivated by this new and wonderful man who has so suddenly appeared. "With enticing words of man's wisdom" he works his way into the hearts of the masses and as a result receives their allegiance.

Heads of nations will become desperate concerning the pressing problems of the day. Mounting distress and perplexity will arise in the area of international economics. Endlessly drawn out cold-war economies will sap the strength of the strongest nations. Deficit spending will pass the peak danger points. Overwhelming national debts will destroy public confidence in their monetary units.

International monetary exchanges will continue to funnel huge amounts of money to the underdeveloped countries. Yet because of their exploding populations these weaker nations will outgrow their food production capacities and remain in relative poverty.

Excessive spending for the economic and military aid around the world will have taken its perilous toll. Foreign-held claims on the gold balances could cause the wealthier nations to collapse financially. In panic, people will surrender their rights to strong leaders who will point to solutions. Fear of chaos will be so great that they will entrust these national leaders with complete power.

The insoluble world conditions will become unbearable. The resources of all nations shall be exhausted. Ominous depressions will threaten to spread rapidly.

In weakened desperation, peace treaties may be signed. Nuclear stockpiles will presumably be destroyed, blockades ended and tariff barriers eliminated in large portions of the world. The common-market philosophy will spread, creating new problems, which will demand unusually gifted leadership to make it successful.

From such a situation, nations shall pool their resources and form an amalgamated empire. Ten nations will federate in an effort to survive. The rulers of these nations shall bend every effort to meet all the needs, but will fail. One of them shall suggest that they consult this gifted, dominant personality that they have been hearing so much about. By logical reasoning they will conclude that only through world dominance by a single leadership will prosperity for all and safety from nuclear war be established.

Haven't they heard that Antichrist has superhuman organizational abilities, and extraordinary power to do the impossible? He has been seen and heard over international TV, and what a forceful speaker he is. Was not his name on every tongue?

The rulers of the ten nations will rise up and overwhelmingly accept the proposal that they hold consultations with this great new man. Why hadn't they thought of this before? They would go to him immediately. This conference promises to change the history of the world! A day never to be forgotten.

Satan exults in this his newest triumph. Is this not the goal toward which he has been working? Had he not been whispering this very same thing in the ears of these very same rulers? Before the great conference convenes, however, a smaller one takes place. This private meeting has two chief participants, Satan and his instrument, the Antichrist. That night, plans are laid and sinister schemes are worked out in preparation for the summit meeting with ten of the great rulers of the world. At last Satan's details are worked out with Antichrist, the messianic counterfeit. The plan is perfectly prepared to ensnare not only the ten rulers who are coming, but all the world. The rulers are ushered into the conference room of the Antichrist, little knowing what the result will finally be.

At once the ten kings are deeply impressed with the superior intelligence of this master man to whom they have come with their urgent problems. They are astounded to find that he already has a definite program worked out that has the markings of a political genius. The plans are laid before them and explained in the minutest detail. It is a superb policy, a superior program. Its workability is seen at once. This is exactly what they need. This policy will cause industry to prosper. (Daniel 8:25.) This program is the work of a genius, and is thus recognized by the ten kings.

Then a decision will be reached. A man with such ingenuity, such sagacity for organization, such a knowledge of financial affairs—a man with all these powers concentrated into one being—this man should be their leader. Yes, they would make him their ruler. They would form an amalgamation with him as its head. "And the ten horns which thou sawest are ten kings, which have received no kingdom as yet; but receive power as kings one hour with the beast. These have one mind, and shall give their power and strength unto the beast" (Revelation 17:12-13).

I do not know just what kind of a program Antichrist will put into action, but, to say the least, it will be superior in every detail. His policy will revolutionize industry, agriculture, commerce, and business. This great character, energized by Satan, will use his capacity and talent for the supernatural to bring prosperity into the world that will approach millennial proportions. Under his skillful supervision, technology will keep pace with the needs of the day. Despite automation, new employment opportunities will increase. Business will take an upswing, and nations will be lifted out of bankruptcy. Financial miracles will be performed. Agriculture shall flourish as never before. Order will be restored; confusion will disappear. Poverty will be erased, want and squalor eliminated, and hard times will be no more. He will be an unusually powerful orator, and his great speeches shall put new life into the masses. They will hail him as the champion of human interests, the hero of all time and the savior of the world.

He will have no equal. His fascinating personality, his eloquence, his remarkable ability, his uncanny ingenuity, his never-ending stream of brilliant accomplishments will be so irresistible to mankind, that they shall be captivated, and will blindly follow him and give him their allegiance. "And the world wondered after the beast."

There are many who are looking for a vicious beastlike ruler to be the Antichrist. But he will never appear in this form. He will be too cunning, too adroit for that. Only in the last three and a half years of his reign will he be revealed as a maddened, infuriated Beast of sin (Daniel 9:27); but his debut will be after the lying wonders of Satan, a friend to the downtrodden, a champion of human interest, a man seeking world peace. ". . . by peace shall destroy many" (Daniel 8:25).

He will be accepted by the masses because of his princely characteristics, his ability to bring order out of chaos and success out of defeat. The world will never willingly accept any ruler who comes forth as a beast. His true nature shall be subtly camouflaged by Satan. Only his brilliance and genius will be revealed to the world in the first part of his reign.

This is why Hitler could never have been the Antichrist. During World War II many religious writers wrote of Hitler as being the Antichrist. But he came as a man of war, a mad beast to destroy free society, defeat the democracies, exterminate the Jews and dominate the whole world. One of his first acts after coming to power was to start a reign of terror against the Jews. His death legions overran nations whose only desire was to remain at peace with the world. Nearly all of Europe fell before his destructive military machine. Consequently, he was the world's most hated man. True allegiance cannot be won by hate. When Hitler started his reign of terror against the Jews and raised his hand against God's ancient people, God put on him a curse. Because, he that blesses Israel shall be blessed and he that curseth Israel shall be cursed. Hitler was doomed.

One of the main features of the policy of Antichrist shall be his unilateral rearmament program. All the nations will agree to disarm. The exception will be Antichrist's army which will control the world, ostensibly for peaceful purposes. Armies will be provided with instruments of destruction. According to Revelation 9:16, it appears that some two hundred million soldiers will take part in the Battle of Armageddon. While verbally crusading for peace, the Antichrist will actually be preparing the world's largest army for his mighty battle to fight against the Son of God.

Sometime, somewhere, during the Tribulation this great character will be mortally wounded. "And I saw one of his heads as it were wounded to death; and his deadly wound was healed . . . the beast which had the wound by a sword, and did live" (Revelation 13:3, 14). These verses suggest to me that this great emperor shall be assassinated, slain by a sword. In death he goes to the place of departed spirits. His body is not yet cold. This is a moment for which Satan has waited centuries. Now is his opportunity. His plans are laid. He is ready. He acts. Away down in the bottomless pit there is that unclothed demon spirit awaiting special assignment. It may be the spirit that led Nimrod to build his tower to high heaven. I do not know. It may be the spirit of Judas Iscariot! Who knows? Judas was called by our Lord, "A son of perdition." Jesus also made this declaration, "good for this man had he never been born." Christ went so far as to say, "One of you is a demon." Paul tells us in 2 Thessalonians 2:3, that the Antichrist is called, "that man of sin, the son of perdition." In Revelation 17:8, he is spoken of as, "the beast that . . . was, and is not; and shall ascend out of the bottomless pit, and go into perdition."

This is all suggestive to me that the Antichrist will be a reincarnation, as well as a resurrected being. It is probable that the voice of Satan shall sound down through the abyss, summoning the demon spirit that has been waiting for centuries. Swiftly, the demon spirit joins its leader. Thus, this spirit, just brought up to enter into the physical body of the assassinated ruler, arises as the man of sin; the son of perdition; the recognized Antichrist of prophecy; the Beast of Revelation 13; a resurrected being.

And then shall commence a period of persecution and suffering so terrible that it will have no parallel in the history of mankind. The persecution heaped upon the people of God in the past will fade away into insignificance when the blasphemous, hideous reign of Antichrist begins. Energized by Satan and with a beast-like disposition he proceeds to blaspheme God, persecute those who missed the Rapture and all that dare to call upon God. (Read 2 Thessalonians 2:1-12 and Daniel 11:36-39.) For the last three and a half years of the Tribulation will be a period in which Antichrist will exalt himself and execute his own will. He will magnify himself above every god, speak terrible things against the God of gods, and prosper until the indignation comes to its end. He will be the most dreaded being that ever walked the earth in the form of a man.

His kingdom shall be like a leopard, a bear and a lion. (Daniel 7:3-8.) So we are reminded of Daniel's four beasts, the leopard, representing Greece; the bear, representing Medo-Persia; and the lion representing Babylon. This fourth beast that John saw will have all the terrible characteristics of these great empires. All their power, brutality, and utter disregard for God shall be concentrated in the man of sin and he shall be the combination of them all.

Antichrist will not stop with merely the rulership of the ten kingdoms that sought his help. These will prove to be a stepping-stone to world domination. Starting with ten nations and as a ruler over an amalgamated empire, he finally will become the military genius who successfully overruns the earth. His conquering legions will span the oceans, and nation after nation will fall. Antichrist eventually will become the world dictator. "And power was given him over all kindreds, and tongues, and nations" (Revelation 13:7). The flag of Antichrist will someday fly over the capitals of each and every world nation. This will include the United States of America.

But the spirit of Antichrist is already in the world. "And this is that spirit of antichrist, whereof ye have heard that it should come; and even now already is it in the world" (1 John 4:3). The spirit of Antichrist is unalterably and eternally opposed to Jesus Christ. This spirit is sweeping around the world inducing men and women to hate God, to deny His existence and to hate righteousness. This rejection will prepare them for the Great Tribulation and the Battle of Armageddon and eternal destruction. It is leading the world to cry, "Away with Christ." But when Christ is turned out of this world, Antichrist will be turned into this world.

But, thank God there is another Spirit sweeping around the world and this is the greater Spirit of Jesus Christ. He is girdling the globe, empowering men and women to quit sin, love righteousness, and serve God. God's Spirit is preparing them for the Rapture, the Marriage Supper of the Lamb, and the Millennium, when the saints rule and reign with the Lord. "Greater is he that is in you, than he that is in the world" (1 John 4:4). If we have the Spirit of God's Son in our hearts we are more than conquerors over sin, for greater is the Spirit of Christ than the spirit of Antichrist. God's power in our lives makes us victorious and triumphant. The spirit of Antichrist cannot lull us to sleep as long as the greater Spirit of Christ rules and reigns in our hearts. This Holy Spirit shall finally cause us to eternally triumph over Antichrist, for when our Saviour comes riding down on the clouds of heaven, He shall defeat Antichrist and all his formidable forces and cast them into hell, where they will defy God no longer.

Friends, are you on the winning side? Do you have the greater Spirit of Christ mastering and managing your heart and life? This is real living, both for time and eternity.

CHAPTER THREE

The False Prophet and the Mark of the Beast

WHAT IS THE MARK OF THE BEAST? How will it appear? Will everyone receive it? Who will be the third actor in the drama of the end-time? Will there be any religious worship in the Tribulation? What is meant by the Great Tribulation?

The Tribulation will be a period of unparalleled suffering involving the whole earth, but especially so for the Jewish people. It will last at least seven years. It will take place immediately after the Lord has raptured His redeemed Bride out of the world. Hence, the world will be left without the presence, power, prayers, and wholesome activities of its most righteous inhabitants. The restraining influence of the Holy Spirit will be gone, the salt of the earth removed. Sin no longer will be curbed or restrained for the Holy Spirit, so long grieved and rejected, shall only passively work with the people that remain on the earth. Earth's holy people will be gone. Think of it! How would you like to live in a city in which God had taken out His redeemed people? Did you ever stop to think what a terrible place this old world will be when its righteous inhabitants are raptured away to the portals of Heaven? I don't want to be here during that time.

It reminds me of my recent trip to Moscow. It was the day before Easter Sunday. I had visited the Kremlin. I had viewed the dead bodies of both Lenin and Stalin before the latter was removed, due to the Russians' de-Stalinization program. I thought of the years these men had spent in stripping the minds of the Russian children and youth of their belief in God. I had not yet met a single person who admitted his belief in God. I thought to myself, *I've not attended church yet. I feel I'm surrounded with unbelief and it's my first time to be in a country so wholly without God. How strong are the demon powers here. How restless, tense and depressed it makes one feel.*

At the American Embassy in Moscow I was told this: "Russia has no place for God in her plans. She is looking to herself and herself alone. She does not ask for people to pray, to read the Bible, to call on God, or to keep spiritual perspective. It is her way to power that she is depending on. Through this she is controlling her people . . . making them work, bringing prosperity and goods to the world market. She is pushing her scientists to bring forth new weapons to destroy those who do not agree with her. She muzzles her churches and teaches her youth that God is a myth and Christianity is a legend. She says that in a few years, after the old die off, her youth will make Russia a country completely without God. It will be a communist paradise in which God has no part."

In a vastly increased manner, the Tribulation will encompass a time when God is ignored, despised, and blasphemed. Sin will be allowed to burst forth in all its evil maturity, and the world will see evidences of wickedness as never before in history. Lawlessness shall break out and have no bounds. It will be the time when Satan is allowed wider license and will exercise power with almost no limitation. He will come forth with only a short time in which to work. He will set out to usurp the power of the Holy God, to pour out his wrath upon those who missed the Rapture and were left behind. He will be obsessed with a burning desire to blot God's name off the earth and exterminate all memories of Christianity. It will be a time when the abyss is unlocked and demons are given the permission to torment men upon the earth, a time when the patience of God is almost exhausted with the extreme wickedness and degeneracy of a sinful race in whom there is no hope. So terrible will be this period of time that men shall seek death but it shall flee from them. (Revelation 9:6.) It will be the most terrible time in the history of the world.

Revelation 13, reveals that during the Tribulation the world will be led by an unholy Satanic trinity. The first and main actor will be Satan, who shall be cast out to the earth when the redeemed Bride goes up. He will counterfeit the Father. Martin Luther once said that the devil is the "ape of God." Satan shall prepare the way for the rising of that monstrous being from the pit that shall be none other than the Antichrist of prophecy. As a man of sin and the son of perdition, the

Antichrist will be a mimicry of the Son of God. Then to complete this diabolical trio, a third actor shall appear who will be the False Prophet, the religious leader of the Tribulation, coming to counterfeit the Holy Spirit. (Revelation 13:11-17.)

The Antichrist shall intervene in the area of politics, commerce and industry, but the False Prophet will come as a religious leader. He will appear in the form of an innocent holy man of religion, working for the betterment of the world. But he will soon prove to be a wolf in sheep's clothing.

A true prophet gets his call and inspiration to preach the gospel from above. But this prophet whom John calls the False Prophet gets his call, inspiration, and power from below. He will be the consummation of all false preachers, prophets, and religious leaders. All the present modernists, deceivers, and false teachers are his forerunners. The power of deception will be increased a thousandfold when he shall come forth with this power to delude the entire world with his false doctrine.

Antichrist will appear in diplomatic circles and will receive the political support of the masses. But political followers are very precarious and fickle, ever-changing in their support and allegiance, for there has never lacked an endless stream of political leaders. The idol of today will be dethroned tomorrow and another will take his place. Because of this Satan will introduce his False Prophet to place the reign of Antichrist on a firmer basis, a more solid foundation. The only thing that is stronger than political support is that allegiance which comes from the religious. Hence, Satan sends his representative of religion into the world to capture and control the spiritual support of the world. This is necessary because all remaining traces of Christianity must be removed completely.

Man has a soul, a spiritual nature. When God breathed into

man the breath of life he became a living soul. The most deep-seated part of man's nature is that desire to worship some-one or something. This religious drive is the strongest faculty in his life. Russia is approaching a half century of atheistic rulership in which there have been three massive antireligious purges which wiped out many lives. In communist classrooms, the existence of God is denied. Books, periodicals and films try to discredit all faiths and lead to complete atheism. Yet in all this, religious belief is still existent in that country. Why? Because the spiritual part of man's life is constantly crying for expression. That beating, sobbing, pounding thing in our bosom can never be silenced. It may be stifled, ham-pered, and even misled, but never, never silenced.

America is greatly indebted to the spiritual faculty in the hearts and lives of its Pilgrim forefathers. They had such a desire to worship God with full liberty of conscience that they crossed the briny deep and came to a new world that they might freely exercise their religious beliefs. This ever-present faculty and desire to worship gave them power, strength, and bravery to face the dangers and hardships of a new world. And whoever rules men spiritually is the real ruler of their lives. The Antichrist will realize that he cannot best per-petuate himself as an earthly ruler unless he gives his subjects an outlet for their spiritual inclinations. He will realize that his reign will be of short duration unless he has a world re-ligion. This is where the third actor of the drama of the end-time will come in. He will come as an angel of light to lead men into a new and better religion as he will call it. He will hail and honor religion. And he will start his campaign for a new world religious order and system. He will inspire the world to worship Antichrist. He will deceitfully present, in authoritarian terms, a religious basis for their wholehearted worship of Antichrist. Because they loved not the truth, they will be completely receptive for the delusion. The False Prophet will discredit the Scriptures and Christ, by exalting the Antichrist as the only one living on earth who has been assassinated by the sword, yet raised from the dead. Further evidence will be given when an image of Antichrist is erected and then given life and speech! (Revelation 13:15.)

Thus the False Prophet shall launch an all-encompassing, irresistible campaign of glorifying and deifying the Antichrist. He will focus attention on his marvelous power and extraordinary ability. He will begin to deify the new ruler and inspire and coerce the world to pay him their religious homage.

"And he exerciseth all the power of the first beast before him" (Revelation 13:12). The first Beast had power over all kindred and tongues and nations and became their political dictator. The False Prophet shall be given the same degree of power over man's religious life as Antichrist was given over their political life. Thus, he becomes their religious dictator. One day the world will wake up and realize that their lives are ruled by two men—politically by Antichrist and spiritually by the False Prophet. Spiritually and physically they shall be held in a deadly grip by Satan's sons from hell.

As a result, religious freedom will disappear from the world. Existing churches will be forced to change their worship of God Almighty to Antichrist, apparently almighty. The Holy Bible shall be declared outdated and a complete delusion. The False Prophet shall replace it with a new one, whose god shall be the Antichrist. It will perhaps have its gospels telling of the miracles and activities of Antichrist. It will be a book whose laws will be made by Satan and it shall command the people to worship the trinity of hell. "And they worshipped the dragon which gave power unto the beast: and they worshipped the beast, saying, Who is like unto the beast? who is able to make war with him?" (Revelation 13:4).

We already have forerunners of the religion of Antichrist in the world today. We have hundreds of false religions. Religions that deny that Jesus Christ is the Son of God. All such religions are preparing the way for that Tribulation religion that shall ascribe its worship to Antichrist. All opposition shall be destroyed by the new dictatorial government of Antichrist. Remaining clergymen will have to preach about and lift up the Antichrist as God or they will be summarily executed and other ministers will be appointed to attend special seminaries in preparation to preach Antichrist and his new religion. This is not difficult to conceive in our current day. In Red China, noncooperative pastors have been subjected to brainwashing, torture, and death, yet those found faithful would not compromise nor deny the true God.

This present world has rejected Chirst so often and so long until it is now almost prepared for this new religion. Worship days are desecrated, God's laws are despised and transgressed the world over. Yes, the world will accept Antichrist!

So here Church and State shall merge. Religion and politics shall join hands. Freedom of the press, of speech and of religion will be a thing of the past. If men and women ever expect to live right and to worship with freedom of conscience, they had better do it now. For when that dreadful day comes, freedom will be abolished and the masses will be forced to worship Antichrist.

The False Prophet shall deceive the world by means of miracles which he shall have power to perform in that day.

Yes, he will be a miracle worker. Miracles have always been the evidence of a person's religious power. By this means faith is begotten in human hearts. When Christ was upon the earth, He proved Himself to be God's only begotten Son by mighty miracles. Jesus broke up funeral processions, robbed the grave of its victims, walked across the wind-swept, storm-tossed Sea of Galilee, healed the sick and afflicted, opened blinded eyes, unstopped deaf ears, made the dumb to sing, and the crippled to walk. By these great miracles many people accepted Him as the Son of the living God and became new creations in Christ. But with Satanic power, the False Prophet shall perform miracles, not in order to lift men out of sin into abundant living, but rather to enslave, debase and destroy them. All the power of the devil will be at his command.

The latter part of Revelation, Chapter 13, tells us that he will have power to call down fire from the skies. Possibly this will take place in one of the world's largest cities. Thousands will be assembled. The sky will be fair and cloudless, the sun shining in all its brilliancy. Suddenly, with out-stretched hands, the False Prophet will speak toward the heavens, and lo, from the clear, blue sky there shall dart forth a ball of blazing fire. As it streaks through the air, men shall see it. When it falls upon the earth, it shall be examined and found to be real fire. The news of this miracle shall be flashed around the world via all media of communications, including world-wide television.

Verses 14 and 15 tells us that he shall cause the people to erect an image to the Antichrist. We have its type in the colossal image that King Nebuchadnezzar had erected in the plain of Dura (Daniel 3:1-6); where people fell down and worshipped the golden image. In all probability Antichrist's image will be erected in Jerusalem. At the dedication of this unusual image, thousands will be gathered from all parts of the globe. Telecasters, radio announcers, newspapermen, and many officials and dignitaries will be there to cover this ceremony. Millions shall be at home viewing the proceedings or listening to their short-wave radios. Antichrist will be there with his illustrious celebrities. The speaker for the great occasion will be none other than the False Prophet. He is there to speak and dedicate the image to the world's greatest character and humanitarian, the Antichrist. He steps out and delivers a great speech. After a purposeful pause, he stretches forth his hand upon the image. Suddenly, to the amazement of all, except Antichrist, he commands the image to speak. Never in the history of the world has life been produced from an inanimate object. Scientists have tried and failed. Only life begets life. Presently, medical scientists in Russia are constantly engaged in research projects to bring the dead back to life without causing brain damage. There has been some limited success with corpses which are categorized as clinical deaths, that is, those who have been medically dead but a few minutes. But any totalitarian power would be ecstatic if it could infuse life into an inanimate object. Right well the False Prophet shall know this. But while the multitude looks on with breathless suspense and the people in their cities and towns view and hear this spectacular event, life comes into this image and to the utter consternation of all, it begins to speak. Why, it's a miracle of miracles! Never has anything like this happened before in the history of the world. It is astonishingly stupendous. The image calls out for the people to bow down and worship Antichrist. Man after man falls prostrate and worships the image. This will be no farce. The image will not speak mechanically. Apparently it will be a real voice. At the command of the False Prophet the world must worship the image and the failure to do so means death, for we are told that he has power, "to cause that as many as would not worship the image of the beast should be killed" (Revelation 13:15).

It is my sincere belief that this image will be wheeled into the temple in Jerusalem which doubtless shall have been rebuilt and reestablished. It shall be put in the temple, the Holy Place, to desecrate its worship to Jehovah God. This is the abomination of desolation of which Jesus speaks in Matthew 24:15-22. When the Jews hear the command to worship the image and shall see it in their temple, standing in the Holy Place, they shall have their eyes opened to the delusions and the deceit of deification attributed to Antichrist. They shall utterly refuse to bow to the image, for it is rooted and grounded into their hearts never to bow to an image or to an idol. Millions of Gentiles shall see that they have been deceived and will also refuse to bow. And from all over the world there will be a turning to God, a rejection of Antichrist and a refusal to worship the image of the Beast. Millions shall see that they have been deceived and shall be converted to Jesus Christ and to full obedience to the true God. In so doing, Jew and Gentile at this point shall incur the wrath of the Antichrist, who, upon seeing their refusal to worship his image shall start a reign of terror that has no parallel in history. The refusal of the Jews to worship the image means that they refuse to accept Antichrist as their Messiah and true God. If one bows, it means that he takes Antichrist to be God. This is essentially the basic decision that faced the three Hebrew children in Nebuchadnezzar's day who had the choice either to bow to his image of gold or to burn in his fiery furnace.

There are two laws in this world that men live by—the law of faith and the law of compromise. We are called upon to compromise and reject the Bible teaching that God has held up as a standard for us to live by in this twentieth century. If we refuse to bow down, if we refuse to compromise our convictions, then we are told we will burn. We will be consumed. We will be set aside. We will have no influence upon the human scene. We will be as nothing. We will be as the off-scouring of society. You will either bow or you will burn. But there's one thing certain. If you bow, if you compromise, if you deviate, if you set aside God's Word which is the way, the truth and the life through Christ, if you compromise, you will ultimately lose what you may gain by compromise. For God teaches, "If you bow, you will burn." If you compromise, you will never keep what you gain by compromise.

Everything we do is by compromise or by faith. Our conviction is put to the test every day. We are called upon to do what we know is right, but the devil will tempt us to compromise in order to gain money or to gain approval of someone we work for or with whom we associate. If we gain that, what do we have? Pretty soon we have lost it.

The three Hebrew children showed their total commitment to God when they faced the dictator and said, "O Nebuchadnezzar, we are not careful to answer thee in this matter. If it be so, our God whom we serve is able to deliver us from the burning fiery furnace, and He will deliver us out of thine hand, O king." He is able. Let weakness lie limp on His shoulder; our God is able. Let the heathen imagine a vain thing; our God is able. Let the kingdoms rage; our God is able. They said, "He is able. But if He doesn't see fit to do it, we may burn in your furnace, but we will not bow to your god."

Where are we in America? Where are we in this twentieth century? Where are we? We are trying to settle our problems ourselves. So many of us have bypassed God. We have left God out of our thoughts. We have let sin creep in. We must be born again. Christ said, "Ye must be born again." You cannot substitute anything for the new birth, though men try. I'm a member of a fine church, perhaps you are, but that is not the new birth. We must repent of our sins and ask God to forgive us of our sins. We must live in the Spirit.

If the smell of fire is on our garments, we will be consumed. Only as we are clean, as we have faith, as we have God at the center of our lives can we stand in the furnace. And the furnace is hot. It is heated seven times hotter. They are coming against us. Communism is only one "ism" in the world. Materialism is perhaps worse than communism. Atheism and all these things are coming at us to throw us in the furnace. We must stand. We may burn, but we won't bow. We will not bow.

In the coming day of Antichrist, he will begin blaspheming the name of God, and will give the command that all who refuse to bow to his image shall be sought out at once and killed. "Death to the traitors! Hunt them down like beasts of the forest! There must be no unbelievers in the world!" His infernal legions of death will comb the cities, the rocks and dens of the mountains, in search of those who refuse to bow to his ultimatum. "Here is the patience of the saints: here are they that keep the commandments of God, and the faith of Jesus" (Revelation 14:12). Those who with conviction and courage turn from the idolatrous image of Antichrist to receive Jesus and keep the commandments of God will face immediate execution or the chance to recant. To worship the Beast's image will be to go into perdition with him. To go to war against the Beast will offer no hope, for if anyone will kill with the sword they shall in this manner be killed. Many will flee into the mountains, the dens and caves of the earth for no mortal will be able to live where the power of the Beast extends without recanting and worshiping his image. The people of God have suffered many persecutions at the hands of the wicked, but all these shall be insignificant in comparison to the intolerable persecution of the Beast. Under Antichrist, persecution shall reach its wicked maturity; hatred of the righteous shall increase a thousandfold. All the power of the devil shall be turned loose upon those who yet fear God. Their lives shall be in jeopardy every moment. Those who have been left behind when Jesus came for his redeemed Bride, the professing but not possessing believers will be tried and tested as never before. From then on it will be a martyr's route to Heaven. "These are they which came out of great tribulation, and have washed their robes, and made them white in the blood of the Lamb" (Revelation 7:14). These are the Tribulation martyrs. They missed the Rapture. But at last, their eyes shall be opened and, refusing to bow to the Antichrist's image, they shall be sought out and killed.

If there ever was a time that people should get on fire for God, it is today. It will be terrible for those who miss the Rapture. Antichrist, the newfound god, will have such power over his followers that they will brand as traitors all who refuse to worship the image. It behooves you and me to be ready for the coming of the Lord, lest we be found unprepared for that sudden event.

During the last of the seven years shall come the most diabolical order ever issued to man, the Mark of the Beast. "He causeth all, both small and great, rich and poor, free and bond, to receive a mark in their right hand or in their foreheads" (Revelation 13:16). This will be included in Antichrist's master plan for bringing prosperity back to the world. This will be a universally recognized mark. It will be the necessary medium of exchange. Equally well known will be Antichrist's name and his number, 666. (Revelation 13:18.)

Now this will be a very beautiful mark. It will be devised by the cunning mind of Antichrist to get the complete allegiance and obedience of the people; and will so tie them to himself until they can never get loose. As the price for settling people's problems and bringing back world prosperity, the Antichrist will demand that they accept his mark to show to the world that they are in allegiance to him. The decree shall be made that unless men take this mark, they will be unable to work and will not be allowed to buy or sell. If not in the forehead, it will be in the right hand because the right hand is a source of contact. In shaking hands, the mark could readily be seen and recognized. In paying a bill, when the money is handed over for it, the mark would easily be identified.

Let us visualize the developing conditions during this totalitarian rule of Antichrist. Shoppers at a supermarket will be requested to show the Mark of the Beast at each checkout counter. No mark, no food. "Sorry, I can't sell you any groceries. If I attempted to do so, my life would be gone within 24 hours." Some couples, still refusing to accept this mark, will become increasingly distressed for their children as the utility companies begin to shut off their services. No heat, no light, no water. The reason? No mark. Where can they turn? Leave the neighborhood, the state, the country? But they cannot sell their homes; they cannot purchase transportation tickets by air, sea, or land. Besides, the same condition prevails throughout the whole earth. There is no way out. An elaborate and thorough espionage system will make evasion virtually impossible. In that day, even brother shall turn against brother and father against son. There will be absolutely no selling or buying without the mark of Antichrist.

The farmer will have his produce confiscated unless he has the mark. The blue-chip stockholder will not be able to buy or sell in the bull or bear market—for him the stocks will be worthless unless he accepts the mark. Manufacturers will try to find a market to sell their tools and machinery, but sales will be forbidden unless the mark is exhibited.

Such is the future for those who are left behind to face Antichrist. Yet, there will be many thousands who will refuse to take the Mark of the Beast. For they will receive the faith of Jesus Christ and love not their lives unto death. (Revelation 12:11.) Far worse than financial ruin, physical deprivation, starvation, or martyrdom will be the alternate judgment for those who do receive the mark of Antichrist. "If any man worship the beast and his image, and receive his mark in his forehead, or in his hand, the same shall drink of the wine of the wrath of God, which is poured out without mixture into the cup of his indignation; and he shall be tormented with fire and brimstone in the presence of the holy angels, and in the presence of the Lamb; And the smoke of their torment ascendeth up for ever and ever: and they have no rest day nor night, who worship the beast and his image, and whosoever receiveth the mark of his name. Here is the patience of the saints: here are they that keep the commandments of God, and the faith of Jesus. And I heard a voice from heaven saying . . . Blessed are the dead which die in the Lord" (Revelation 14:9-13).

Through the concerted efforts of the treacherous trinity of Satan, Antichrist, and the False Prophet, the Great Tribulation will reach its climax. But at last the limit is reached. The diabolical reign of the Antichrist comes to a close. Christ returns! And with the brightness of His coming, Antichrist and his vast armies will be destroyed at the Battle of Armageddon. To the lake of fire, burning with brimstone, will Antichrist be consigned, along with the False Prophet, there to endure the full penalty of their rebellion. (Revelation 19:20.)

At the same time a special angel will come to do God's bidding. "And I saw an angel come down from heaven, having the key to the bottomless pit and a great chain in his hand. And he laid hold on the dragon, that old serpent, which is the Devil, and Satan, and bound him a thousand years. And cast him into the bottomless pit and shut him up, and set a seal upon him, that he should deceive the nations no more, till the thousand years should be fulfilled: and after that he must be loosed a little season" (Revelation 20:1-3).

Thus the Millennium will begin as Jesus Christ takes over the reins of world government and will rule the world in peace and righteousness as King on David's throne. And then, along with the Twelve Apostles, all of the redeemed who have faithfully served Him during their earthly sojourn, will reign with

Him. Christ shall reign as King of kings and Lord of lords. For a thousand consecutive years, this earth will be governed in righteousness by the followers of Jesus. With Satan bound, sin curbed, war abolished, Christ on the throne, righteousness shall fill the earth as the waters cover the sea and the desert will fully bloom and blossom as the rose. Glory to God!

I urge you, choose Christ and choose Him now. Earth's history is approaching its finale. Sin and wickedness are to be dethroned forevermore. Get ready now for that blessed day in which the redeemed will live and reign with Jesus Christ forever. Let us heed the prophetic warnings. Let us hold fast to the "sure word of prophecy."

CHAPTER FOUR

Will the Bride of Christ Go Through the Tribulation?

IS THE BRIDE OF CHRIST scheduled to go through the Tribulation? Must the faithful taste of Tribulation horrors? Will Jesus come before or after the Tribulation? Is there any hope to escape the dread night of Tribulation?

There are many who teach that the Bride of Christ will have to go through at least a part of the Tribulation, if not all. If the saints are going to be forced to go through the Tribulation, it would be better for them to die now than to live until Jesus comes. So fearful will be the terror of the Tribulation, that it would be best for the saints to be buried in the cemetery—resting beneath the sod and the flowers, their spirits with the Lord in glory, awaiting the dawn of the Resurrection Morning—than to be living here on the earth during the Tribulation Days.

If it is true that the Bride must go through the Tribulation, I pray, let me not live till Jesus comes. Let me die before the Rapture. Then I shall, by death, escape the Tribulation and have part in the First Resurrection. Let me die now, if the storm of the Tribulation is about to break! If the saints must go through the Tribulation, then the only way that the Lord of glory has of delivering His people, will be by death. God forbid.

But thank God, the saints are *not* going to have to go through the Tribulation but are scheduled to go up before it begins! The Lord encourages the faithful Christians with these words, "Because thou hast kept the word of my patience, I also will keep thee from the hour of temptation, which shall come upon all the world, to try them that dwell upon the earth. Behold, I come quickly: hold that fast which thou hast, that no man take thy crown" (Revelation 3:10, 11).

Before the awful storm of the Tribulation shall break in upon the earth, those who are living for Christ and are looking for His appearance shall be suddenly caught away to meet the Lord in the air. They shall be safely above the storm. This does not mean that the faithful saints of God will never have to go through hard trials or bitter persecutions. Even now in several parts of the world, persecution is being heaped upon those who profess Christ as their Saviour. I suffer persecution constantly. I know many others who suffer also. But the Bible teaches, clearly and emphatically, that the Bride will miss the entire Tribulation Period by being raptured above it, in the coming of the Lord Jesus Christ.

What saith the Scriptures? What will be the relation of Christ's coming to the Tribulation? The Second Coming of

Christ is divided into two stages; first, His Rapture and then at the close of the Tribulation which shall last at least seven years, His Revelation. His Rapture, which is known as the "catching away of the Bride," is a supernatural appearance. It is Christ suddenly, and only for a moment, appearing in the air. At that time He will not come to the earth. At the precise moment chosen by God for Christ to appear, not everyone in this world will see Him, only those who are looking for Him. Those who are in Christ will see Him, whether they are asleep or awake, for He will appear on their consciousness. He will be seen by their eyes, and in the flash of a second there will be a raising of the righteous dead and a translation of the righteous living. His Revelation, however, is known as that time when He comes back to the earth with His saints to fight the Battle of Armageddon, to destroy Antichrist with the brightness of His glory and to set up His millennial reign on the earth. Intervening between the Rapture and the Revelation is the Tribulation Period. Many are frightened when the coming of Christ is mentioned. They are either misinformed on this great subject or there is something wrong with their spiritual experience. They generally associate the events that shall transpire at His Revelation with those that shall transpire in His Rapture. The Rapture is before the Tribulation and the Revelation shall close the Tribulation. In the Rapture He comes *for* His saints, and in the Revelation He comes *with* His saints. Therefore, remember that He cannot come with His saints until He first has come for His saints. The one naturally precedes the other.

Study the following outline and you will readily see that the Lord is coming both before and after the Great Tribulation.

"Rapture," or secret coming for His saints.	"Revelation," or public coming with His saints.
Secretly. "As a thief." Revelation 16:15; Luke 17:34-37.	Publicly, "Every eye shall see Him." Revelation 1:7; Zechariah 12:10.
Coming for His saints. 2 Thessalonians 2:1; 1 Thessalonians 4:14-17.	Coming with His saints. Colossians 3:4; Jude 14, 15; Revelation 19:8-14; Zechariah 14:4-5.
Coming "In the Air." The world will not see Him. 1 Thessalonians 4:17.	Comes down to earth, "His feet standing on Mt. Olives." Zechariah 14:4.
Coming "before the Great Tribulation." Revelation 3:10; Luke 21:36.	Coming after Great Tribulation. Matthew 24:29-30; Revelation 19:11-16.
Coming "in the Rapture" as the Blessed Hope. Titus 2:13.	Coming in the Revelation "with great wrath." 2 Thessalonians 1:7-9.

Thus, before the Tribulation He comes for His Bride, and at the close He returns to the earth with His Bride to then set up His millennial reign.

The Bride will be caught away before the Great Tribulation Period ever begins. Antichrist cannot be revealed until the Bride has been lifted physically out of the world. This is very clear in the teaching of the Apostle Paul, "And now ye know what withholdeth [i.e., restrains the Antichrist] that he might be revealed in his time. For the mystery of iniquity [the trend toward Antichrist] doth already work: only he who now letteth [restraineth] will let [continue to restrain], until he be taken out of the way. And then [when the one that restrains is taken out of the way] shall that Wicked [the Antichrist] be revealed" (2 Thessalonians 2:6-8). In other words, there is a power in this world that is restraining the power and influence of sin and evil. That power is stronger than the power of Satan. This power is in the world curbing lawlessness and hindering the public presentation of Antichrist. What restraining power is this? Is it political power? No, there is no earthly power greater than the power of the devil. For as prince of the power of the air, he controls principalities, powers, and rulers. (Ephesians 2:2; 6:12.) There is one power in the world greater than the power of the devil. That is the power of the Holy Spirit. "Greater is he that is in you, than he that is in the world" (1 John 4:4). During the Tribulation the earthly ministry of the omnipresent Holy Spirit will, for the greater part, be passive instead of active.

We are now in the dispensation of the Holy Ghost. His advent into the world, dispensationally, was on the Day of Pentecost. The disciples of the Early Church could not do without the power of the Holy Spirit. Christ closed them down for "spiritual repairs" by ordering them to go to the Upper Room to receive power from on high. He said, "Behold I send the promise of my Father upon you: but tarry ye in the city of Jerusalem, until ye be endued with power from on high" (Luke 24:49). Jesus further explained, "Ye shall receive power, after that the Holy Ghost is come upon you: and ye shall be witnesses unto me" (Acts 1:8). The moment you receive the baptism with the Holy Ghost as they received it on the Day of Pentecost according to Acts 2:4, you are supernaturally endued with power from on high. It is not the kind of power which moves machines or turns on lights—no, that is left for human beings to develop. The baptism with the Holy Spirit brings another kind of power—power that dwells within us and which we feel inside us. Christ described the power of the Holy Ghost as a river of water flowing out of our inner-most being (John 7:38, 39)—a powerful, rushing stream—irresistible, glorious—sweeping all opposing forces from its path.

Christ promised that this power would come "after that the Holy Ghost is come upon you." When you are saved, you receive power to become a child of God. (John 1:12.) The experience of sanctification brings the power of cleansing and consecration. It is in the baptism with the Holy Spirit—and only after you have received the Spirit in this experience—that this greater power for service and witnessing comes upon you.

From the day that Peter and the other disciples received the baptism with the Holy Ghost, their lives were controlled by the Holy Ghost. He acted as their administrator and manager. Peter, who denied the Lord, stood up and preached. Thomas, who doubted, went forth to carry a message of faith to a whole nation. John, one of the "sons of thunder," became the Apostle of Love.

According to Jesus Himself, it was better for the Apostles after they received the baptism with the Holy Spirit than it was when they had Christ with them in the flesh. When Christ was here in the flesh, He could not be beside each of them always. He could not control them fully. Actually, while He was on the earth in the flesh, control of the disciples was ultimately lost. When He was arrested, they all left Him and fled. When He was tried, Peter denied Him, and Judas committed suicide. When Jesus died, in panic they all ran to hide for fear of probable death. After His resurrection He found them behind barred doors in terror.

After these same disciples received the baptism with the Holy Spirit, their lives were stabilized as the great Administrator personally took charge of them. They left the Upper Room and came down to preach to multitudes in the city. They filled Jerusalem with their doctrine. The judges and rulers could never quench their spirit. They turned the Roman Empire upside down as they carried the light of God's truth into every darkened corner of the universe.

When the Holy Spirit has completed His mission of gathering out the faithful believers from among the nations, He will be taken out of the way as a restrainer. His active presence, through consecrated lives of Spirit-filled men and women now in this world, keeps lawlessness and godlessness within certain bounds as a great dam or seawall holds back the turbulent waters. But when the Holy Spirit, as the restrainer, ceases to restrain, He will take the fruit of His mission, the Bride, to her heavenly Bridegroom, where she will forever be with the Lord. He, the heavenly Eleazer, will bring the Bride, the heavenly Rebecca to the heavenly Isaac, the Lord Jesus Christ. (Genesis 24:67.)

Many years ago in our community there was a boy who fell in love with a girl whose parents would not allow the boy and the girl to court. One day, when the boy was there, the father ordered the boy off his premises and told him never to return. That did not stop the courtship. It stopped them being together for a while. But they had a friend, who became their go-between. And they wrote love notes. Their love grew until one day he sent her a note asking her to elope with him. She agreed. They set the night. Long after her family had gone to sleep she was wide-awake. That evening she had slipped on her wedding garment and over that, an old housedress. Her family was not suspicious. But all the time they were asleep she was sitting at the window waiting. She did not know the exact moment. She only knew that sometime that night he would tap on the window. When he did, she just slipped off the old housedress. There she was, dressed to go. He helped her and they went away in the cover of night. The next morning the father called for his daughter to come down and cook breakfast. When she did not answer, he had a premonition and went up the stairs to find that she had gone. When he found them, they were married.

Similarly, the Holy Spirit has been bringing us the Lord's messages and taking our messages to the Lord. And our love has been growing and ripening and maturing until we're ready. Every man and woman and child must get ready and stay ready. You must wear the conditions of this life as you wear a coat. Something that you can take off at any time. You must not wear them too closely to you. You must not let the affairs of this world get too close to you. You must have a relationship with this world, like your coat has to your body, that you could just slip off and go right up. You must wear it as a loose garment. It is later than you think. But, oh, the joy of being ready to meet Him, and of seeing Him in His person.

The Holy Spirit will not leave this earth, deserting God's people, leaving them to the terrors of the Great Tribulation. Rather, He will take them out of this sin-cursed world to meet Jesus in the sky. So shall they be saved from Tribulation horrors.

When the Bride is caught up, then the offensive warfare of the Church will cease. The Holy Spirit will only work in a passive manner, as a wooing agent. The distinct difference in the work of the Holy Spirit after the Rapture and during the Tribulation is that He will no longer be the restrainer of the

Antichrist spirit. But individuals, who are under the awful Antichrist reign, will yet have opportunity to repent if they have not received the mark, that their souls might be saved even though they suffer martyrdom.

The Scriptures clearly reveal that there will be many people saved in the Great Tribulation. John saw such a number, and mention is made of them in Revelation 7:9-14. But, oh! what a time of suffering they will experience by failing to be ready for the Rapture.

Jesus warned in Luke 21:36, "Watch ye therefore, and pray always, that ye may be accounted worthy to escape all these things that shall come to pass, and to stand before the Son of man." There is a way of escape. By watching and praying and wholly following the Lord, we will escape all these terrible things that are destined to come to pass upon the earth.

To further prove that God hath not appointed His people unto wrath, but will call them away before the Tribulation, note Matthew 24:28 and Luke 17:37, "Wheresoever the body is, thither will the eagles be gathered together." The body represents Christ, and the eagles refer to the alerted saints. There are some who reject this idea because this body denotes death, and eagles are birds of prey. But Jesus is pre-eminently the Saviour because of His ignominious death. It is by His descent that we rise and by His death that we live. "Except ye eat of my flesh and drink of my blood ye have no life in you" (John 6:53-55). He is the Lamb slain from the foundation of the world and His body is that upon which all true saints feed. Therefore, since we, as the people of God, receive our life from His flesh and blood, we are like unto eagles. As eagles of faith we feed on His broken body and shed blood. Eagles are royal birds which have a strange wisdom, remarkable eyesight and swiftness of flight to gather wheresoever the body is. So are those who have their spiritual senses alerted, for "unto him shall the gathering of the people be" (Genesis 49:10). Eagles are exceedingly strong on wing and build their nests among the hills, the insurmountable mountains and inaccessible crags, and fly above the storm before it breaks. In a spiritual sense, all these characteristics are possessed by the saints. Hence, wheresoever the body of Christ is, there shall the eagle saints be gathered. But when? Before the storm? The eagles have regular watchtowers from which they keep a constant vigil. When the thunders peal and the lightnings flash, the eagle gets ready for a flight. And, amidst the rolling thunder and the gathering shadows, she bares her breast and flies right into the storm; and the same winds that bring the storm upon the earth, take the eagle above the storm, where she bathes and basks in the pure sunlight until the storm is over. When the storm has subsided she returns to her lofty home. Such is the picture of the Coming of the Lord for His Bride in the Rapture. As the Tribulation approaches, the saints shall mount their lookout towers and scan the horizon for a glimpse of their Saviour. They will read the signs of the times, watch the storm clouds of Antichrist appear and, as all this intensifies, the saints will get into the closet of prayer and hear Christ say, "Surely I come quickly." Her quick response will be, "Amen. Even so, come, Lord Jesus" (Revelation 22:20).

Just before Antichrist steps out on the scene, the redeemed shall rise. Just before the storm of the Tribulation breaks in upon the earth with all its intensity to try the earth dwellers to the uttermost, the redeemed shall rise. Before the Mark of the Beast is made the medium of exchange, the redeemed shall rise. Before Satan is turned loose on the world, the redeemed shall rise. Before sin shall reach its final and wicked maturity, the redeemed shall rise. The eastern skies shall be split asunder by the majestic form of the Son of God, as He comes shouting and crying, "Come my people, enter thou into thy chambers, and shut thy doors about thee: hide thyself as it were for a little moment, until the indignation be overpast" (Isaiah 26:20). And from all over this old sin-cursed, devil-ridden, hell-bound world, the Bible-reading, blood-washed, Spirit-filled, Christ-loving, God-serving, faithful band of holy people, from Abel's day to this, shall bid good-bye to earth's sorrows and woes. Bidding defiance to decay and gravitation, the redeemed "shall be changed, in a moment, in the twinkling of an eye, at the last trump: for the trumpet shall sound, and the dead shall be raised incorruptible. Then we which are alive and remain shall be caught up together with them in the clouds, to meet the Lord in the air: and so shall we ever be with the Lord" (1 Corinthians 15:52; 1 Thessalonians 4:17). What a flight! The rapid release of the underground Minuteman Missiles and the underwater Polaris Missiles are not to be compared with the instant rising of the dead in Christ from graves under earth and sea. The 18,000-mile-per-hour speed of the astronauts' capsules will seem to decelerate as millions of saints rush past at a speed greater than light to meet the Lord Jesus Christ in the skies!

Amidst the bursting graves of the dead in Christ, and the shouting of those who are resurrected and translated, the bridal company shall meet in the clouds and shall follow their Lord into the heavens, and through the pearly gates. They shall appear before the Judgment Seat of Christ, where on the basis of each believer's work on earth, rewards shall be granted. The Bride shall then be presented to the heavenly Bridegroom in the Father's house and together they shall eat the Marriage Supper of the Lamb. (2 Corinthians 5:8-10; 1 Corinthians 3:11-15; Revelation 19:7-9.) It thrills my heart with joy unspeakable to think of God's provision to remove His people from the Tribulation horrors. So whether we live till that time or die before, we shall rise with our blessed Lord before the Tribulation.

Meanwhile the Tribulation Period will be raging upon the earth. Antichrist is blaspheming, and the devil is walking about with unbridled liberty, damning souls forever. Men are seeking death and finding it not. Millions are tasting Tribulation horrors. Do you want to miss the Tribulation? Are you longing to be in the marriage company at the Marriage Supper of the Lamb? Then you must sever relations with this ungodly world, deny yourself worldly lusts, and wholly follow the Lord. Are you ready should Christ come today? You can be.

When you belong to the Lord, how comforting is the thought of the Second Coming. Paul wrote, "Wherefore, comfort one another with these words" (1 Thessalonians 4:18). The early Christians greeted each other with the word, "Maranatha," which means *the Lord cometh*. They were comforted when persecution confronted them on every hand. The thrones of the kings of that day mattered little in comparison with the throne of their King and Lord. For long centuries, the true Church has waited. But now, at last, His coming draws nigh. Let us live in love, courage and calm certainty. Let us plan our tomorrows so that we can best serve Christ faithfully for decades to come. Yet let us so live each day that we shall be prepared for the sudden appearance of our Lord. Maranatha! The Lord cometh!

CHAPTER FIVE

The Jews in Prophecy

WHEN THE COURT PREACHER was asked by Frederick the Great to give, in one word, an unanswerable proof for the inspiration of the Bible, he replied, "The Jew, Your Majesty." Since the time Abraham was called to leave Ur of the Chaldees to become the first Jew, God has in a special way dealt with and through this ancient nation to bless the world. For this reason, Satan has made Israel his primary target, ever assaulting the Jewish people in order to annihilate them.

Israel, in rebellion and disobedience to God, has experienced suffering exceeding that of other less enlightened nations. "But he that knew not, and did commit things worthy of stripes, shall be beaten with few stripes. For unto whomsoever much is given, of him shall be much required" (Luke 12:48). Israel, in obedience, has been exalted as no other nation, with God-given prophets, priests and kings. They are still His people, and a God-planned destiny yet awaits them.

Think of how much we owe them! Our Bible came from the Jewish people. Our Saviour, the Lord Jesus Christ Himself, was of Jewish lineage. Let us never forget that. Jewish blood flowed in His veins. Peter, John, Paul, and all the rest of the inspired writers, save one, Luke, were Jewish! The Jews are God's first people. They were the first to serve Him. They are the seed of Abraham and the good olive tree. They have wandered away from God but His covenant yet remains and will be carried out, through a faithful remnant. (Romans 11.) They are beloved of God for the Father's sake. God has not cast away His ancient people, and today it is evident that God is preparing their hearts for the acceptance of Jesus Christ at His Second Coming. This will be the fulfillment of His covenant. The Jews will then believe in the name of the only begotten Son of God—the only condition that God accepts from either Jew or Gentile.

No race has suffered such unspeakable outrages, impoverishment, racial hatred, or frightful persecutions as have the Jewish people. Scattered among the nations—slaughtered like so many sheep, beaten, abused and driven from pillar to post—the Jews have survived to this day. Diabolical schemes have been devised to exterminate them from the earth. Think of the near success of the Pharaoh, Assyrians, Nebuchadnezzar, Haman, Antiochus Epiphanes, Titus and 20th century Hitler! The last was the worst. Some one-third of the world's Jews were slaughtered at the hands of the Nazi regime; six-million human beings. Six-million Jews who were segregated from their dwellings, thrown into ghettos, humiliated, turned into slave workers, starved and tortured before being destroyed in extermination traps such as Buchenwald, Dachau and Auschwitz.

The dreaded Gestapo spread its dragnet over most of Europe under orders of sadistic, perverted, insatiable men such as Eichmann. As many as 18,000 Jewish men, women and children were killed daily. They were hounded, tormented, massacred. Their wives and daughters were violated; their synagogues sacked, their scrolls—the tablets of the Law—defiled. Here and there were some heroic Europeans who risked the wrath of the Nazi Secret Police. Somehow, 200,000 Jewish refugees were hidden, kept alive in their homes or smuggled to safety. Even in Hitler's headquarter city of Berlin, 5,000 Jewish people remained alive to the war's end. The same amount survived in Warsaw. If ever the desire for a homeland was strong, the Jews felt it then. If ever world sympathy was awakened to favor arrangements for the Jewish people to possess a homeland, it was during World War II.

In Luke 21:29-33; Matthew 24:32-35, Jesus compared the Jewish nation to a fig tree. He said that when the fig tree begins to bud we are approaching the end-time. The budding of the fig tree is a type of the Jewish people returning to their homeland which was promised to Abraham and to his seed. Read what God says, "And he shall set up an ensign for the nations, and shall assemble the outcasts of Israel, and gather together the dispersed of Judah from the four corners of the earth" (Isaiah 11:12). "Therefore, behold, the days come, saith the Lord, that they shall no more say, the Lord liveth, which brought up the children of Israel out of the land of Egypt. But, the Lord liveth, which brought up and which led the seed of the house of Israel out of the north country, and from all countries whither I had driven them; and they shall dwell in their own land" (Jeremiah 23:7-8). "And I will bring again the captivity of my people of Israel, and they shall build the waste cities, and inhabit them . . . And I will plant them upon their land, and they shall no more be pulled up out of their land which I have given them, saith the Lord thy God" (Amos 9:14-15). Notice in these Scriptures how that God has decreed that when His people would be so cruelly treated that they became "outcasts," driven out of the nations, exiled —then He would gather these outcasts and bring them back to the homeland, Palestine.

Why to Palestine? Why this strange and sacred little corner of the earth? Because Palestine has been the home of the Jewish people from Bible times unto this day. God gave it to them. Palestine is situated at a point of unusual geographic, historic, and political interest—past, present, and future. It has been called the crossroads of the nations. As a narrow strip of coast along the eastern end of the Mediterranean, it is a link between the Arabian Peninsula on one side and Asia Minor on the other. By virtue of this position, it has been the highway and the bridge between the most ancient seats of civilization. It has become a station on the great lanes of international traffic. It is the most central and promising spot on earth. God had chosen this most strategic land in the world as the homeland of His people. And God has been allowing racial hatred and bitter persecution and spoiling of the Jewish people for the expressed purpose of gathering them back to Palestine.

Palestine was once a land flowing with milk and honey, satisfying a population of more than three million. In AD 70, Titus and his Roman army beseiged Jerusalem, destroyed the temple, and slaughtered hundreds of thousands of Jewish people. After six decades of revolt after which all pockets of resistance were wiped out, desolation set into the land as the people of Israel scattered in all directions. Throughout the long centuries, although much suffering was experienced during the Frankish Crusades, the Spanish Inquisition, the ghettos and pogroms of Europe, many Jews still held to the hope of someday returning to Palestine.

At the close of the nineteenth century, amidst fiery new outbreaks of anti-Semitism in Europe, the Jewish people again experienced a deep longing for the homeland. Several thousands left Eastern Europe, left its rejection and persecution of them, to join some 25,000 Jews who were living in Palestine. Shortly thereafter, Theodor Herzl spearheaded the Zionist movement in order to have world Jewry find a home in Palestine, secured by public law. Because of the ingenious discovery of the noted chemist, Dr. Chaim Weizmann, Great Britain in gratitude to this Jewish man pledged her aid in establishing Palestine as an official Jewish State. This was publicized in the Balfour Declaration in 1917. By this time, some 75,000 Jewish people lived in Palestine.

Then came the thrilling report of General Allenby's capture of the Holy City on December 11, 1917. Without firing a shot, without artillery destruction, Jerusalem was delivered from the Turks, who had fled. Quietly and without blare of trumpet, General Edmund Allenby, Commander in Chief of the Allied Armies in the East, entered the city of Jerusalem.

Under the four century reign of the Turks, and the preceding centuries of rule by the nomadic Arabs, the once beautiful and fertile land of Palestine had become barren and desolate. But the fig tree began to bud as thousands of Jewish people prepared to pour into Palestine when the League of Nations effected a British mandate over Palestine in 1923. Leaders of Zionism met with Arab rulers, and purchased poor, barren land from Arab owners at a price far above its value. Jewish immigration continued to increase, especially as Hitler's shadow started to fall across Europe. By the time World War II began, there were over 500,000 Jewish people in Palestine, who labored diligently to make the land productive. However, the Arabs who had sold the desolate land demanded that it be returned after seeing the vast changes. Basic, long-standing problems continued to exist. The Arabs claim all of Palestine as their homeland and so do the Jews. They both claim to be offspring of Abraham. In fact, the Mosque of Omar is built on the traditional site of Solomon's Temple. Many of the places sacred to the Jewish people are owned by the Arabs, who forbid the Jews to visit them. The Arabs think that the Jews have come to run them out of their own land. There is bitter strife between the two races.

The Arabs are descendants of Ishmael, while the Jews are descendants of Isaac, and God said, "In Isaac shall thy seed be called" (Romans 9:7). In Palestine we have the same feud that existed between Isaac and Ishmael. (Genesis 21:9-12.) It was with Isaac and his seed that God established the everlasting covenant. (Genesis 17:19.)

During World War II, the Zionists cooperated fully with the Allies against the hated fascist enemy. In various British formations, 25,000 Jews were recruited and Jewish units served in several campaigns. Their European brethren did not have such opportunities. In Eastern Europe, the Nazis exploited the traditional anti-Semitism of the peasants, so that no aid would reach the Jews. Their extermination continued in major ghettos

of Poland, under the fanatical supervision of Eichmann. Brave
Jewish risings took place against overwhelming odds. Thousands of young Jewish people joined the various undergroun ˙
resistance movements.

The *blitzkrieg* warfare of the Nazis sped their armies to th
English Channel. Strangely enough, instead of invading England, Hitler opened a second front and sent many divisions to
the very gates of Russia's largest cities. But the tide was turning. D-Day arrived and France was invaded by the Allies.
The Nazi forces were driven back into Germany. Finally,
VE-Day arrived on May 6, 1945, when unconditional surrender
was signed by the Germans.

The slaughter of six-million Jewish people in Hitler's Europe
aroused world-wide sympathy for the Jews. It was now im-
perative that Israel have its own homeland to which the
scattered, unwanted refugees could go. World Jewry had been
reduced from 17 million in 1939, to 11 million in 1945. But
God brought good out of evil. Favorable events shaped up
rapidly. The problem of Palestine was turned over to the
newly formed United Nations. In the fall of 1947, the United
Nations General Assembly adopted a majority recommenda-
tion. Palestine would be divided into a Jewish state and an
Arab state. Britain's mandate would end in six months.

On May 14, 1948, as the last British soldier left Palestine,
the Jewish National Council and the Zionist Council at Tel
Aviv proclaimed the establishment of the Jewish State of
Israel. After 1,900 long years, the despised, dispersed Jewish
people could return home. The greatest exodus since the days
of Moses could now begin. Israel would give world Jewry
the right of immigration in order to gather in the exiles. All
restrictions were abolished.

The infant nation Israel, under the leadership of its first President, Dr. Chaim Weizmann and Prime Minister David Ben-Gurion, saw the flag of David lifted for the first time since Titus removed it in AD 70.

Many people thought that the new state of Israel would never survive conditions of bankruptcy, war and the circle of hostile Arabs. But the world has seen an infant nation sustain every trial and yet grow stronger.

It has been my privilege to personally observe the growth and changes of Israel during three visits to the Holy Land. I met the people of Israel in their homes and fields; I interviewed their leaders and spoke to people who have come to Israel from almost a hundred nations. I asked each one: "Why did you come to Israel? Have you come to meet the Messiah?" I will try to give you some of their answers.

There is a feeling akin to awe that sweeps over me when I step on the soil of Israel. My entire being seems to vibrate with the presence of God. Seeing the people, as they plant and rebuild the land, makes me realize that I am at grips with a miracle. For I am seeing . . . hearing . . . feeling the mighty things God is doing in that tiny land on the edge of man's wilderness.

The people made a terrific impact upon my spirit. They have stopped running—they have come home! They have suffered murder, sorrow and humiliation for two thousand years; still through the centuries, scattered to the far reaches of the earth, they have clung to the worship of the one God. They have outlived everyone who has tried to destroy them. Now they are taking the land of Israel again in the same way and spirit of Joshua . . . foot by foot, hill by hill, town by town. This is the spirit of the land of Israel and I have been drawn irresistibly under its spell.

From the first moment, when we were met by a high-government official at the Lydda Airport, until my personal interview with the Prime Minister, Mr. David Ben-Gurion, the hand of the Lord was upon our mission. I give glory to the Lord for the extraordinary things we were able to accomplish there. No Christian minister could go into a country like Israel and be given the privileges accorded our group without the help of God. Israel does not accept Jesus as the Messiah (Christ) as we do. They are cordial and friendly to Christians; they acknowledge Jesus as a prophet; but they do not accept Him as the Son of God.

For about 1,500 years the name Jesus was seldom mentioned among the Jews and few Jewish writers wrote about Him. But a great change is taking place. His name is more or less freely used both in books and conversation. Great Jewish scholars, in the United States, England and Israel, have written about Him at length and have produced sketches of His life, so that today He is rapidly being recognized as a great religious teacher by leading Jewish people the world over. In a conversation I had with a prominent Jewish man in our nation's capital, the name of Jesus and Christianity was used very freely. It is evident that God is moving among the Jewish people in an effort to prepare them for the reception of Jesus Christ as their Messiah.

A great spiritual experience awaited me at Capernaum, where I began the first stage of my most recent visit to Israel. How picturesque Capernaum is, situated on the northern rim of the Sea of Galilee, with its grand old trees casting their shadows across the ancient ruins. Here God gave me the privilege of preaching to more than 100 Jewish men and women who came to hear me. They had taken a boat at Tiberias and sailed across the sea much as the people did 2,000 years ago to hear Jesus. It was a moving experience to see them get off the boat and come through the trees toward the remains of the synagogue where Jesus used to preach and heal. I did not have to think what to say. My heart was full of Jesus in that sacred place. I told them what Jesus had done there . . . of His great miracles of healing.

A great anointing was upon me as I pointed to the ruins and read them Jesus' prophecy: "And thou, Capernaum, which art exalted unto heaven, shalt be brought down to hell: for if the mighty works, which have been done in thee, had been done in Sodom, it would have remained until this day. But I say unto you, That it shall be more tolerable for the land of Sodom in the day of judgment, than for thee."

"This scene of desolation," I told them, "is a reminder to every living human being to respect the visitation of God. We, too, will find our houses, our cities, our souls left desolate if we do not open our hearts to God's visitation."

I don't know exactly how to describe it, but that crowd of Israelis really received my message. One woman from Russia said, "Reverend Roberts, we don't accept Jesus as you do, but we know Jesus loved the people."

Back in 1952 I saw very few large trees in Israel. Now, thousands of acres were virtual forests. And they are beautiful. The people are planting millions of new trees annually. It is done principally by the children, who are taught by their parents to love the land of Israel.

I had the privilege of planting a banana tree. Somehow in

the act and process of planting a tree I seemed not only to capture the spirit of Israel but actually to become possessed by it. I was made acutely aware of the deep, moving forces—the human forces of faith, confidence and expectancy.

When a tree is planted, it is pointed toward the future . . . not what it is now, but what it will become. And the Israelis believe joyously and confidently in the future. Many of them realize they don't have time to make a life for themselves, so they are building for tomorrow—pouring all of their love, knowledge and understanding into the hearts and minds of their children.

In one *kibbutz* I had the privilege of talking to a young teacher and his wife. In America this man could command a good salary, for he is brilliantly educated. There he receives only a small sum. But they have a greater motivation and satisfaction than money. There is the opportunity to train 650,000 children now registered in Israeli schools. This number equals the total population of Israel at its birth. The room of the young teacher was poorly furnished, but when he walks out of that room to teach the little boys and girls, he walks out proudly. Israeli teachers give themselves untiringly to their work with joy and deep satisfaction.

I spent quite some time with this young man. He was friendly and responsive.

"Do you look for the Messiah?" I asked.

"I am not religious," he answered. But I soon understood that his words meant, *I am not of the Orthodox Jewish faith.* He was not a strict follower of the Talmud—a collection of Jewish traditions.

"Do you believe in miracles?" I asked.

"No," he answered. He did not believe that the Red Sea had

opened for Moses, nor that the walls of Jericho had fallen miraculously. But I found that he did believe in miracles—the miracles of science, the miracle of the rebirth of his nation.

"But these are miracles we create with our hands," he said. "We work in the fields; we drive the big tractors; we plant and cultivate; we harvest and transform our land. The women work right alongside the men. And these are things we believe in."

"Well, you do believe in miracles," I said. "Now, may I give you my testimony?"

"Please do," he said politely, his eyes reserved and cautious.

Then I told him how I had been so desperately sick, how God had saved and healed me of tuberculosis and a stammering tongue. I told him how God had spoken to me and called me to preach and had told me to take the message of His healing power to my generation.

He listened quietly, then more intently. Finally, he seemed to be hanging upon every word, "Do you believe me?" I asked.

"Yes," he answered. "I do!" And he began to open up, and I realized that God had touched his heart.

The kibbutz where this couple lived is called Ein Gev. It is what we would call "a community" in America. It is a settlement where about 500 families from 50 countries live closely together, sharing mutual interests and work. They farm the fields together and eat together, and all the earnings go into one treasury. There are many *kibbutzim* in Israel.

During the earlier fighting nearly every building of this kibbutz was wiped out, but the people simply moved underground and kept working. They built underground shelters where they lived with their families and children. Here they had their printing presses, their kitchens, their beds and their belongings. For six months they slipped out during the day to farm and fight and crawled back at night for rest and shelter. Even now they have deep trenches dug from their homes to these shelters, so that in case of attack they can reach protection quickly.

As I looked around me, I could see what the young teacher meant. These Israelis are not afraid. They know they are going to succeed. Their faith is unshakable; they believe in their future.

As I traveled in Israel, I became impressed with the health and general well-being of the Jewish people.

"Dr. Mann," I asked one of the most famous physicians in the world, "how do you account for the good health of the Jewish people?"

This great doctor, who discovered the cure for silicosis (a disease of the lungs which afflicts miners), smiled proudly. "Reverend Roberts, it is truly remarkable," he said. "As you know, these people came from everywhere. Once, more than 5,000 suffering from infectious tuberculosis were brought in at one time. I was truly frightened. I didn't know what to do. But the strangest thing took place. The very moment these people set foot on the soil of Israel, something happened inside them. They began to get well quickly. Our doctors and our nurses moved into their tents and worked with them, showering their love and attention upon them. The people responded. I almost believe they would have recovered without treatment. Today, we have only 800 bed patients in all of Israel with tuberculosis. My answer is 'I believe God did it!'"

I asked this great physician, "Dr. Mann, do you believe that God heals?"

"I most certainly do," he answered, "and I believe almost every doctor will tell you the same thing. I believe God heals because I have seen it with my own eyes."

I felt very privileged to interview Dr. Mann. He heads the staff of Hadassah Hospital, a new $20-million institution in Israel which soon will be graduating 1,000 doctors a year. So the work of mercy and medical care continues to expand in Israel.

The events of my visit to Israel moved fast and had great variety. It is impossible to recount all of it—there is too much. The most unusual people I saw and visited were the Yemenite Jewish people.

They came from the land of Yemen at the southern tip of Arabia, on the Red Sea. They are believed to have migrated there in King Solomon's day. For these thousands of years they have lived in Yemen, cut off from the outside world. Until 1948 they had never seen a modern convenience—an automobile, a train, an airplane, an electric light, a water faucet or anything of a modern nature.

Throughout the hundreds of years they have suffered great persecutions. They lived in ghettos, but their religion has been kept the same as it was in King Solomon's day. I talked to Yemenites who told me that they had copied the Bible from Genesis to Malachi by hand, exactly as people did in Jesus day. If they made one error, they would tear it all up and start over.

Most of the Yemenites, being cut off from educational facilities, got their education by memorizing the entire Old Testament. I talked to Yemenites who had memorized every word in the Old Testament.

The isolation of the Yemenite Jews continued until 1948,

when God spoke to their leaders and caused them to organize an exodus from Arabia to Palestine. Israel's Prime Minister, David Ben-Gurion, called upon the United States government to help, and cargo planes were dispatched to the Port of Aden, controlled by the British, to bring the Yemenites to their ancient homeland.

The only way they could possibly get to the Port of Aden was to walk—so they walked! Some of them walked 1,000 miles over deserts and mountains. Sometimes they traveled in 120 degree heat, sometimes in freezing temperatures.

The Israeli government sent film crews down to film this great exodus. I saw the films of this pilgrimage. I saw where some had died. I heard little children crying for water. They stumbled on, and some fell, but you could hear the Rabbis saying in strangely vibrant tones, "Take another step, little children. We are going home to meet Messiah." Somehow they put one foot in front of the other and stumbled on and on.

When Mr. Ben-Gurion sent his messengers saying, "We're going to send airplanes for you," the Yemenite Jews did not know what an airplane was. When they saw the planes, they refused to get on board until their Rabbis read from the prophecy of Isaiah that God would send for them and bear them home on the wings of an eagle.

The Rabbis told them, "Little ones, God is sending His eagles for His children." Then these little Yemenite Jewish people climbed on without any fear at all. Some of the women gave birth to their babies while in flight, but there was not the loss of a single child. More than 50,000 Yemenite Jews came home to Israel in this great airlift.

When they reached Israel, some got off and kissed the ground. The authorities put them aboard buses. They had never seen a bus before and they expected it to fly. When it didn't, they were disappointed. But they had come home.

I visited one Yemenite family. The yard was filled with happy, friendly little children. All of the neighborhood was there.

We went into the kitchen and sat around the kitchen table, covered with the most beautiful tablecloth I ever saw. One of the sons translated for his father, an old Rabbi, 85 years of age, with a long beard, flashing eyes and a very kind face.

I said, "Ask him what his dream is . . . what he wants most in the world."

The Rabbi answered, through his son, "I want three things: first, I want to see Israel developed; second, I want to live long enough to see peace; third, I want to see Messiah with my own eyes."

I had looked forward to my interview with Israel's Prime Minister with much anticipation. My appointment with him had been set at 9:30 AM, but it was 5:00 PM before I was able to see him. Several other appointments were canceled that day because of a political crisis. But he still made room for me and graciously received me. Several government officials sat with me from 9:30 that morning until 5:00 in the afternoon because they wanted to assure me of my welcome as a guest of the government of Israel. As I entered the Prime Minister's office, before I could be seated, he took my breath away by asking this first question: "Mr. Roberts, as a Christian evangelist, what are you trying to do with people? I don't mean what are you trying to get them to believe, but what are you trying to get them to be and to do?"

Mr. Ben-Gurion is a little man, probably no more than 5 feet 3 inches tall. His hair is completely white and stands out stiffly around his head. He has luminous eyes and wonderfully expressive hands and face. His glance is penetrating—he seems almost to read your thoughts. I was taken by surprise at this question, but the Lord gave me this answer before I could really think about it:

"I am trying to get people to love each other," I said. "I am teaching people that they cannot love God without also loving their fellowman."

Mr. Ben-Gurion smiled and said, "Mr. Roberts, that's a good answer. "But," he continued, "love is not enough. People have needs. There can be no equality among people until those needs are met. Do you agree?"

I said, "Yes, I believe that love must be translated into action. That is what Jesus taught."

He said, "That's right."

We talked about human needs, about people who didn't have decent housing, adequate clothes or sufficient food. He said, "Love becomes an empty word unless you meet the needs of these people."

I said, "Yes, I believe God comes to meet the needs of people. He comes in the form of their needs."

"That's right," he agreed. Finally he said, "Mr. Roberts, we love the Bible, too."

"Mr. Ben-Gurion, what part has the Bible had to do with the rebirth of Israel?" I asked him.

"Everything!" was his ready response. "Without the Bible we could have done nothing. The Bible said we would return to this land. We have come home. The Bible said we would rebuild the land. We are rebuilding it. The Bible said we would plant the land. We are planting it."

And I knew it was true, for I had been all over the land,

seeing it blossoming like the rose. This is why almost 1½ million Jewish people could return to this land in its first 15 years of statehood. By 1970, Israel expects to have a population of 3 million.

Then I presented the Prime Minister with one of our Bibles, a beautiful white-covered copy, with both New and Old Testaments in the Hebrew language.

I said, "Would you accept this as a token of the love of the Christian people who also love Israel?"

"Mr. Roberts," he said, "I will be very proud to have it."

Then I wrote the inscription, "May the blessing of the Bible be upon you, Mr. Prime Minister, and upon the people of Israel." He read to me in the Hebrew Bible and then it was time for me to go.

My last question was, "Mr. Ben-Gurion, what is your dream for Israel?"

Almost spontaneously, he replied, "I want Israel to be an example to other nations of love, freedom and dedication. And I want Israel to be as the Prophet Jeremiah says, 'a light to all nations.' "

I then prayed with the Prime Minister and took my leave.

Thus ended the most memorable event of my visit to Israel as a guest of its government.

When I departed from Israel, I did not lose the spell that had fallen over me. Even now I feel the surge, the rise, the swell, the thrill of deep emotion. There is something going on in Israel. It is of eternal consequence, and the spiritual significance of that something leaps in my blood like a flame. God's ancient people are carving out an empire. They are literally creating it with their own hands. That's what the Bible told us they would do. The meaning of it in terms of a coming great world revival and the Second Coming of Jesus has thrilled me to the very fiber and core of my being. You and I are having a tremendous part to play in this last powerful drama of the end-time.

In connection with this, I must tell you about our Hebrew Bibles and the part they are playing in this great epic. As you know, the Oral Roberts Evangelistic Association is printing the complete Bible in Hebrew, both Old and New Testaments, under one cover, and distributing it free to the Jewish people around the world. Dr. Myron Sackett directs this work. Wherever I went in Israel, I found our Hebrew Bibles. In schools, in libraries, in the Hebrew University, in homes; everywhere, I found them. They are printed in the pure Hebrew language and, as such, are welcomed by the Jewish people as reading and study material. Our purpose is to help the Jewish people learn about Jesus, the true Messiah, and this is the way that they learn about Him.

We have distributed over 100,000 Hebrew Bibles, but many more are needed. They must be placed in homes, in schools, in kibbutzim, in libraries, in universities. Revival will not come to Israel until the people read the Bible. We must sow the land down with Hebrew Bibles. The Jewish people must learn about Jesus of Nazareth. They will not listen to the usual preaching but they will read these Bibles printed in pure Hebrew. The language has been restored to popular usage. The Old Testament is taught in public schools and in universities. The New Testament is read as religious literature, although presently not considered on the same level as the Old Testament by Orthodox Jews. The person of Jesus still disturbs the searching hearts among the Israelis. For others, these Bibles may not be read for six months or even six years, but one of these days, God's time will come. And when it does, thousands of Jews will pick up the Bibles which have lain unused in their homes. They will open and read, and God will give them light and understanding. They will realize that Jesus is the true Messiah, and revival will come like a mighty rain upon the earth.

What a thrill! What a challenge! God has selected you and me to stand at a pivotal point in human history. The stage is set, the clock is wound and the hand of destiny is moving toward us.

Again, I say, God did not choose the Jewish people because they were weak and would run from danger. For these 2,000 years they have borne the brunt of sorrow and humiliation. They have been killed by the multiplied millions. They have been scattered like the wind across the vast face of this earth. Still they have clung to the ONE God. They have outlived everyone who has tried to destroy them. Now they have come home. This little land, chosen by the Jewish people situated on the edge of man's wilderness, has become again the cross-roads of the world.

This is where God wants His ancient people to be. On this frontier they are to rebuild the land and live out their torments and fear until that long awaited day when they are ready to cry out, "Blessed is he who cometh in the name of the Lord!" I believe our Hebrew Bibles are a powerful witness for that day and a vital key to its glorious dawning. That day cannot be far off. It is very near at hand.

Before that day arrives, however, the temple will be re-built. This is a subject that lies close to the heart of every Orthodox Jew in the world, and especially in Israel. Preliminary work has been going on for sometime in preparation for the building of the temple itself. You may ask, why is it not in the process of building now? Why such a delay when so many Jewish people are established in Israel? The answer to that question lies to a great extent with the Arabs. Jerusalem is a city divided in two parts. The traditional site of the Temple of Solomon is occupied by the Mosque of Omar. It may not be necessary for the temple to be built on this spot but it seems probable. However, we know that the temple will be built somewhere in Jerusalem, for it will be desecrated by the Antichrist.

What will be the relation of the Jews to the Antichrist? Will they receive him? Undoubtedly. They will play a leading part in the Tribulation and the drama of the end-time. In fact, the Bible reveals that Israel's regathering is necessary in order for the Tribulation to occur. (Jeremiah 30:6, 7.) Primarily, the Tribulation will be the "time of Jacob's trouble," a time in which the Jewish people shall go through experiences far worse than ever before.

Israel will have great prosperity (Amos 9:11-15), so much so that they will fall prey to the nations who will come to seek spoil. (Ezekiel 38:1-12; Joel 2:18-22.)

Already, Israel is the scene of amazing transformations. Swamplands have become flourishing fields. Sand dunes have given place to beautiful orange groves. By 1965, Israel expects to start shipping 4 million crates of citrus fruit out of the new modern Mediterranean Port of Ashdod, which is expected to house 150,000 inhabitants. Only 15 years old, Israel constantly furnishes agricultural, medical, scientific and educational assistance to the lesser-developed nations in Africa,

Asia and Latin America. With no iron ore, Israel has developed a structural concrete which makes the construction of 20-story buildings possible, with hardly a steel girder.

There is untold wealth in the Dead Sea and Negev desert areas. Recently, a $2½-billion development program was announced. This will include industry, electric power, mining and housing in southern Negev. Israel's overall economy is growing rapidly. Jerusalem, Tel Aviv and Haifa are prosperous modern cities. The Middle East contains immense reserves in oil and chemicals. When Antichrist rises, he will realize the strategic, political, economic and religious position of Israel. One of the first things that he shall do will be to win the confidence of the Jewish people, inspire their homage and convince them that he is their Messiah. Daniel 9:27 reveals the fact that he will make a covenant with them at the beginning of the seven years of his reign. This alliance is one in which Israel makes "a covenant with death, and with hell are we at agreement" (Isaiah 28:15). Jesus said, "I am come in my Father's name, and ye receive me not, if another come in his own name, him ye will receive" (John 5:43). Why did not the Jews accept Jesus as their Messiah? Jesus came in an entirely different manner than He was expected. The Jews were expecting the "Lion" out of the tribe of Judah, and Jesus came as a "bleeding Lamb," slain from the foundation of the world; they looked for a financial wizard, but at one time Jesus had to depend on the fish to pay His taxes; they dreamed of a conqueror that would break the iron rule of Rome and exalt them to the skies, but Jesus constantly cried, "My kingdom is not of this world"; and finally allowed a Roman procurator to sentence Him to a shameful death at Calvary. But Antichrist will meet their requirements. He shall recognize their national aspirations, give them greater prestige, allow them special privileges, more firmly establish them in Israel. If the temple is not already built, he will aid them in its erec- tion, restore its worship, and allow them to offer daily sac- rifices. Thus at his inception of rulership, representatives of Israel will go to the council room of the Antichrist. They will agree to sign this covenant for seven years.

Three and a half years shall pass by in which everything shall work to the advantage of the Jews. They will be realizing an age-old ambition. The land will be further transformed under the skill and resources of the Jews. But in the midst of the seven years—the middle of the week, according to Daniel —this is what will happen, "And in the midst of the week he [the Antichrist] shall cause the sacrifice and the oblation to cease, and for the overspreading of abominations he shall make it desolate, even until the consummation, and that determined shall be poured upon the desolate" (Daniel 9:27).

Only three and a half years will have passed by when the Antichrist—now the undisputed world dictator, and false Messiah—will have a colossal image made of himself, and sent to Jerusalem to be placed in the temple. Through his False Prophet he shall demand that the Jewish sacrifices cease and that all Jewish people must fall down and worship his image. (2 Thessalonians 2:3, 4; Matthew 24:15-22; Revelation 13:14-15.) This is what is known as, "The abomination of desolation," namely, the blasphemous assumption of Deity by the Beast. It is that dread hour when Antichrist will go to the temple of Jerusalem, stop the sacrifices, proclaim himself God, and demand the worship of the people. Then will every Israeli have his eyes opened. He will know that he has been deceived. The commandment, "Thou shalt not make unto thee any graven image," will immediately flash in his mind, and he will refuse, absolutely, to bow down to the image, or worship the Antichrist.

And then will the fires of the Great Tribulation break upon the Jewish people in all its fury. Neither man nor woman will be spared. On every side they will be commanded to fall down and worship the Antichrist. Upon refusal, they shall be slain like so many sheep with the exception of those who shall be fortunate enough to escape to the mountain fastnesses. It is in this way that Antichrist will begin his reign of terror that will have no parallel in the world's history. Former persecutions will not compare to the relentless persecution and terrible reign of death of the Antichrist. When Antichrist sees their rejection of his claims, he will resolve not merely to run them out of the country but to exterminate them from the earth. Whereas Hitler's dragnet drew in one third of the Jewish people for slaughter, the Antichrist will increase the ratio.

Hence, the command to flee. There won't be a moment to lose. Until they get out from under his influence and far away from his death legions, they will be slaughtered in their unbelief. In anticipation of that terrible time of "Jacob's trouble" Jesus says, "Then let them which be in Judea flee into the mountains: Let him which is on the housetop not come down to take any thing out of his house: Neither let him which is in the field return back to take his clothes" (Matthew 24:16-18). There will be nothing saved except life. Household goods and property will be confiscated. "And woe unto them that are with child, and to them that give suck in those days!" Yes, for they will be greatly hampered in their flight. "But pray ye that your flight be not in the winter, neither on the sabbath day." It will be cold in the mountains and death from exposure would be the result. And, if it be on the Sabbath day, it would mean that the Orthodox Jews, who adhere strictly to the Law of Moses, will not be able to flee farther than two miles; and that will be insufficient distance to be safe from the wrath of Antichrist. Oh, what suffering it will mean to the helpless Jews. Jesus states further, "And then shall be great tribulations such as was not since the beginning of the world" (Matthew 24:15-22). Desolation, indeed, will be the order of the day when the wrath of Antichrist is poured out upon the Jewish nation.

We have a type of this in the desecration of the temple by Antiochus Epiphanes, one of the last rulers of Greece, who, in 168 BC, offered a sow on the altar in Jerusalem and compelled the Jewish people to eat swine's flesh. He massacred no less than 60,000 Jewish people in Jerusalem alone. The Jews received a false report that this vicious ruler had been killed. Naturally, they rejoiced, but when Antiochus heard of it he became so angry that he ordered his soldiers to totally slaughter the people. This is but a pale type of the Antichrist who will slay the Israelis without mercy during the Great Tribulation.

The last and only remaining hope of the Jews shall be swept from them. Their first three and a half years of comparative freedom will be swept from them, and Antichrist will plunder them and their land. Oh, if the Jewish people could only see this. If they could read the signs of the times and believe the Scriptures. Christ was not the only one who spoke of it, but Daniel, their own beloved prophet, went into detail describing the horrors and atrocities of that day. If they could see that they are going back to Israel to some day accept Antichrist and experience the Great Tribulation—if they could just see that—perhaps they would wake up and be prepared.

What will be the result? Will Antichrist exterminate the Jews, as will be his avowed purpose? No, the Jewish people will never be exterminated nor lose their identity. They have a God-planned destiny and will yet exalt the name of the true Messiah, Jesus Christ.

There will be a mass exodus out of Jerusalem and Israel at the abomination of desolation. They shall realize that they have been deceived and that Antichrist is an impostor. They shall flee to the mountain fastnesses of that country. There is scarcely another country that has such hiding places. Especially south of Jerusalem, in the region of Petra, are places where one could probably hide for months and months and never be found. A leading Jewish man, who has been through this Petra district many times, informed me that its safeholds were impenetrable and one could hide amidst its caves and dens for an indefinite time without fear of being found. The Arabs have hidden there, and from ambush they carried on their terrorism against the pioneering Jews. Among these hidden places, the fleeing Jewish people shall find refuge.

In this connection I would like to give some very interesting information of the way God is working in advance of such an event. William E. Blackstone, author of the book, *Jesus is Coming Soon,* carried on a very interesting work among the Jewish people, especially in Palestine. Mr. Blackstone died in 1935 at the age of 94, but before his death he had a revelation from God that many of the fleeing Jewish people, awakened to their awful betrayal at the hands of the Antichrist, would find refuge in the dens and caves of the mountain fastnesses around Petra. Out of a $5-million trust fund, Dr. Blackstone in 1935, sent a corps of Christian workers to Petra with great

cases of Hebrew Bibles, encased in copper boxes. They were
sealed in hewn-out vaults in the mountain side of the Petra
region against the day when, according to the Bible, the Jews
will flee from Jerusalem to the Petra Mountain. In the midst
of the Great Tribulation, these Bibles with marked passages
will be found, tracing the lineage of Christ, and the working
and deceit of Antichrist will be exposed to the persecuted
Israelis. These marked passages will show the Jewish people
how they have been deceived, betrayed by the Antichrist, and
that Jesus Christ is truly their Messiah, their only hope. Only
the future will reveal the results of this unique venture of Dr.
Blackstone. Undoubtedly God is mysteriously working, even
now, for the opportune moment when His Word will be a
direct medium in opening the eyes of His Ancient people who
have been in spiritual blindness so long. That is why we have
distributed over 100,000 Hebrew Bibles. That is why we must
continue. (We are doing some unusual things in our Hebrew
Bible work that I am not free to discuss at this time; a work
that I feel will help Jewish souls accept Christ as Messiah
when He comes the second time.)

In our day, the Eichmann trial reveals the total depravity of
cultured, educated man apart from the saving grace and delivering power of God through Jesus Christ. Nazi theologians
tried to deny Christ's Jewishness in order to formulate an all-
Aryan Christianity. After the trial which lasted four months
and included 113 sessions, Eichmann was found guilty as one
of the fiendish, fanatical followers of the Fuehrer. The de-
votee of the crooked swastika cross was executed, his body
cremated and cast into the Mediterranean Sea. But the demon
spirits, which drove Titus and Hitler to inhuman actions full
of venomous hatred, are causing a resurgence of anti-Semitism

to develop all over the world. In Moscow the synagogue was stoned, windows broken. In Germany—even in the U.S.—the Nazi symbol is daubed on synagogues and threatening letters are sent to prominent Jewish leaders.

Driven, humiliated, persecuted—the Jewish people at last shall realize that true peace and real security are to be found only in the Holy One of Israel, who "came unto his own and his own received him not." God will raise up leaders among them, especially the two witnesses (Revelation 11:3-12) who will, as true prophets, have the testimony of Jesus. (Revelation 19:10.) In the caves and dens of the earth the Jewish people will realize that they have been deceived, they will realize that they have rejected their own beloved Messiah. "And I will pour upon the house of David, and upon the inhabitants of Jerusalem, the spirit of grace and of supplications: and they shall look upon me whom they have pierced and they shall mourn for him" (Zechariah 12:10).

In the midst of Tribulation horrors, the Jews shall moan for Jesus. God says, "Alas! for that day is great, so that none is like it, it is even the time of Jacob's trouble, but he shall be saved out of it." God shall hear their cries, see their tears, accept their repentance and deliver them.

After seven years, Antichrist's insane reign will come to an abrupt, dramatic end. Jesus Christ, the King of kings and Lord of lords, will return. And with the brightness of His glory He shall destroy Antichrist and his defiant armies at the Battle of Armageddon. (Revelation 16:13, 14, 16; Revelation 19:11-21.)

And, because they shall accept Jesus Christ as their Saviour and Messiah, the Jewish people shall be intimately identified with Christ in the Millennium. Thank God, at last their long bitter night of blindness, unbelief and persecution will be over. Their acceptance of Christ will exalt them and with Christ they shall rule and reign in righteousness. Hail the blessed hour!